For Jodi

Love.

Lora Kristoff

CM

Behind Closed Doors

The Path of Alzheimers

LORA KRISTOFF

BALBOA
PRESS
A DIVISION OF HAY HOUSE

Copyright © 2019 Lora Kristoff.

All rights reserved. No part of this book may be used or reproduced by any means, graphic, electronic, or mechanical, including photocopying, recording, taping or by any information storage retrieval system without the written permission of the author except in the case of brief quotations embodied in critical articles and reviews.

Balboa Press books may be ordered through booksellers or by contacting:

Balboa Press
A Division of Hay House
1663 Liberty Drive
Bloomington, IN 47403
www.balboapress.com
1 (877) 407-4847

Because of the dynamic nature of the Internet, any web addresses or links contained in this book may have changed since publication and may no longer be valid. The views expressed in this work are solely those of the author and do not necessarily reflect the views of the publisher, and the publisher hereby disclaims any responsibility for them.

The author of this book does not dispense medical advice or prescribe the use of any technique as a form of treatment for physical, emotional, or medical problems without the advice of a physician, either directly or indirectly. The intent of the author is only to offer information of a general nature to help you in your quest for emotional and spiritual well-being. In the event you use any of the information in this book for yourself, which is your constitutional right, the author and the publisher assume no responsibility for your actions.

Any people depicted in stock imagery provided by Getty Images are models, and such images are being used for illustrative purposes only. Certain stock imagery © Getty Images.

Print information available on the last page.

ISBN: 978-1-9822-3451-5 (sc)
ISBN: 978-1-9822-3452-2 (e)

Balboa Press rev. date: 09/05/2019

Preface

I wish to make this very clear.

All situations related in the following pages are described as I viewed our world. None are meant to be derogatory and are expressed solely from my personal emotional perspective.

It is hoped that, should one be facing a similar diagnosis that each page will provide a sense of purpose to continue along the journey that is being laid out before you.

Prayer and strength, in just putting one foot ahead of the other, will carry you through.

Introduction

I am usually a very private person. This experience and the resources I have been able to read have all helped me through some very difficult times. Because of this, I write and reveal what went on "Behind Closed Doors" since there are others, I am sure, that are struggling as I have, and will, hopefully, see that there is a silver lining and things will get better. I read somewhere when you feel you are at the end of your rope…tie a knot and hang on…..(Theodore Roosevelt)

Background

John and I have been together since 1969, after his separation from Betty and her return with her parents to Germany, leaving him, thankfully, with their two children, Jonathan (14 years) and Amy (6 years).

We fell deeply in love and raising two children was welcomed by me, 23 years old at the time. John was an electrician and I, a school teacher. Our lives were filled with work, studies, soccer, hockey, swimming lessons, piano lessons, gymnastics, birthday parties, the German club, travel, our cottage, visits to Toledo and later to Mertle Beach, where John's parents lived. He was a strict disciplinarian with our son and the opposite with our daughter (something I tried to remedy, but failed.) Both love him dearly. The fortunate thing is that we had identical work ethics, beliefs about finances and we worked and saved and worked and saved etc. We were more than generous with our children over the years. Jonathan went off to university in 1974. Amy gave us challenges as a teen, but we survived. We helped them through marriages, divorces, car purchases, home buying home renovations, etc. It seemed like we were a strong unit that could survive anything.

The diagnosis of Alzheimer's came November 17, 2006.

I think the hardest part is saying goodbye to life as we know it. Nothing will ever be the same.

It wasn't completely a shock as I had noticed the changes over time that could not be denied. Losing things, forgetting names, forgetting familiar routes in our neighborhood, these all came on so gradually like dreams that drift in and out of one's consciousness.

The doctor prescribed Reminyl, a fairly new drug that is supposed to cause the nerve impulses to have an extra boost as the brain cells try to talk to one another. The lowest dose had no side effects so we gradually moved up to the 24mg per day dosage. Actually we weren't quite finished with the lower 16mg prescription when I realized John needed a stronger "charge".

My Journal

The first few days....

November 18 2006 ♥

The diagnosis came yesterday. Mood swings happened regularly and John seems anxious when I go anywhere. My feelings are mixed even though he doesn't seem to grasp the concept of this diagnosis. Do I tell anyone? Do I tell the children? They have a right to know. Will the new medication work? How do I keep him active and mentally alert as long as possible? One day he has tears because he appreciates me, next day, he brings up some incident that happened 3 years ago and he doesn't speak to me for hours, always unpredictable.

November 19 2006 ♥

I am pleased he likes word find puzzles. John says his head feels clearer with the meds. I emailed Jonathan and told him- I don't know if that was wise. He is quite distant and problems are still there for him so perhaps I shouldn't have given him more to carry. The other side is, he may feel hurt if I hadn't said anything to him. I don't know how to break it to Amy. She is so happy. I hate to dampen her spirits. My reaction is anxiety and a need to clean, of all things. I want to get rid of the clutter around the house and put everything in order…perhaps trying to get control when I sense it may be lost. We all went out for my birthday dinner with Bert and Mary. I told Amy and Rodney, privately. When we got home, John withdrew, angry, for what reason, I don't know. I just knew to stay clear of him while he sorted it out.

November 21 ♥

I received two calls about Uncle Jim's finances and John went into a tirade about how I was wasting my time with helping him. Uncle

Jim, age 96, wanted to finalize his funeral arrangements and find the "best deal" he could… that is just who he is. John didn't want me gone all day in the city, shouting at me. He tries to control by intimidation and I have to walk away. There is no logic or reasoning anymore. I must do more research to understand and cope with what is here and what lies ahead.

November 22, 2006 ♥

My birthday, started out as a generally good day apart from a search for pens and glasses.

Spoke too soon. His mood changed at 10pm, with another Uncle Jim argument.

November 23, 2006 ♥

We went to Amy's for Thanksgiving Dinner. John was very critical of Rodney's wine, bringing it up over and over again. Changing the subject didn't work this time. We left early.

I have made a promise to myself to find the Alzheimer's Chapter and get busy understanding everything I can as soon as possible. The man I married is disappearing before my eyes. One moment he is there, kind and thoughtful and the next he is angry at the world and anyone he deems may have crossed him. The one closest gets the brunt of anger. Discussion has gone and I just agree or stay out of the way as much as possible. Reading helps, and putting my thoughts and feelings on paper, helps me let go of the hurt I feel.

December 2006 – May 2007 ♥

We went to Florida and we had a very good winter. I was constantly keeping him busy with golf and different projects each day and apart from always shadowing me, all went well. Mood swings were manageable and I began learning how to cope with strange behavior. We saw little of Jonathan and Anna due to their busy lives. I am very concerned about his driving ability and risky actions when on our bicycles. He crossed Federal Highway on bicycle between stop signs and was angry with me when I would wait for the light to change. Everything was always my fault. I know social convention is starting to falter. When at the Golden Coral, a local buffet, he would loudly say, "that one has been here too many times." I tried to choose seats that were away from others as often as I could. I offered to drive most of the way home to ensure our safety. I spent my days agreeing with everything, smoothing every experience in anticipation of outbursts, anger, sadness, paranoia and fear of everything that seemed to challenge his path. It was exhausting.

July 2007 ♥

We had been at our cottage for a week with all the family and had quite a lot of company so the noise and activity levels had been quite high. Robbie, our grandson, a hyper sort, had corrected my husband John's use of "Ella" as the dog's name, for Bella, Robbie being correct. It hit an angry chord with him and he made a lunge for Robbie. Fortunately he was quick and missed the brunt of John's aggression. It all happened so fast, seeing it from across the room, caught me completely off guard. I realized the safety of the children had to be protected as there was no cause for the episode. In normal conditions, whatever that is, recognizing his error would have been the order of the day. This was definitely a change for the worse.

I realized at that moment large family gatherings were too much for him and I had to put their interests first.

It saddens me that this part of my life is disappearing also.

He is very anxious whenever I am away and always says I have taken too much time when running errands so I can no longer relax and browse anymore. He often speaks of "ending it all".

Today he forgot how to spell the word "the" and told me to write a note of explanation to our son following an outburst, while fishing. He hurt our son's feelings and repeatedly reminded him of the mistakes he felt he had made in his past. He was most insistent that the message must be conveyed, although I knew it was not helpful.

This is not a good father son bonding activity to say the least. The note attempted to explain his calling our son's first wife and earlier girlfriends losers. Our son took it as an insult to him, as being a failure in his father's eyes. It rests now that they are avoiding contact, and who knows how long it will last. My role of peacemaker has prevailed over the years and now it must kick into high gear.

I am writing this to sort out my feelings and provide some emotional release in order that I will be able to proceed with as much objectivity as possible. I hope it will work.

It is now July 2007 so it has been seven months already.

I am pleased that John enjoys golfing that will be a life saver for the months to come.

Driving home from the cottage he became disoriented as we drove past the city. Fortunately I was driving and I reviewed our route. I find each day I go over the plan for the day, so we establish a kind of a routine that is comfortable. I find I must repeat the plan a couple of times, being sure it is retained.

I hope the stronger meds will help.

I've noticed that he is quick to anger, a fierce anger, however it subsides rapidly as well and he forgets what upset him in the first place. My response is, no response to anger, let it pass and change the subject.

I had a good day to-day as I had lunch with some girlfriends. It was a mini vacation for me and one I plan on repeating, on a regular basis.

I find he is forgetting normal activities, such as flushing the toilet, something he would never have done in the past. He repeats stories over and over. I found out later that that is the way they try to hold onto their reality. He is insistent that belts should go in the front hall closet and hats should go upstairs. I just agree. He is quick to give his opinion and becomes angry if you chose to oppose him in any way. My response has become "Everyone is different and that is ok." Fortunately our close friends Bert and Mary have been told and are very patient and understanding, Bert seems to be the one that can lift his spirits.

I know he is repeating himself a great deal while golfing at the club and I am not sure who I should say anything to. I don't want to talk about him to others however I want them to have patience with him at the same time.

This is a dilemma.

Aug. 2 2007 ♥

Today he flew off the handle when I said I had told him something and he said I had not, in fact I had mentioned this topic twice (whether or not I was to water the neighbor's flowers) rather a trivial item, so when he spoke to me harshly, it wasn't normal.

We went golfing with a large group today and he kept repeating the stories over and over again. I took Nancy aside and told her what was happening and she said she had wondered about it and appreciated me telling her. I thanked them for their patience.

Another thing that has started, perhaps it has been going on for a while, he feels he must keep talking all the time when we are with others. At home he is quiet and while out, seems to need attention and be somewhat the center of conversations. Personally, I prefer to listen to others and hear about their lives and experiences.

Aug. 22 2007 ♥

He has been happy the last little while and so I don't think I'll start with the anti-depressants the doctor gave us, the mood swings haven't been as prevalent and I don't want to go to the lower dose of the Reminyl and take a chance there will be a further loss in memory. I am still repeating things over and over for him and I am getting used to it. To have him relaxed, it is great. We are heading up to the cottage for four days with friends and I hope he doesn't get stressed out with all the activity. I plan to play everything low key so I hope he will follow my lead. Stress is something he can't cope with.

The situation with Jonathan doesn't help as he brings it up frequently. I know it is on his mind a great deal.

Sept. 2 '07 ♥

John has been having a lot of headaches so he decided not to take the Reminyl anymore. I explained the ramifications and he just said having headaches all the time is worse for him. I guess I have to respect his feelings in that regard. Still no appointment has been made with Dr. Bernard. I'll try again tomorrow.

Nov. 15 '07 ♥

We are heading south on Sunday, things are about the same. Angry outbursts from time to time and he searches me out to fight. I have begun agreeing with him just to avoid the combat. The same issues are brought up again and again. He doesn't realize that his negativity hurts others. Bert has been so patient.

The headaches have stopped however he says he still feels cobwebs in his head. He forgets what we have done the same day and asks when I bought something even though he was with me at the grocery store.

I know I will have to take care of myself to get through this. He has threatened suicide a number of times as he doesn't want to go on. This tends to get my attention, I think, he does it whenever I plan time out with my girlfriends and he tells me they are more important than he is.

I plan to get some good reading so I can escape mentally at least.

Dec 2007 - May 2008 ♥

He has had a relatively good winter. We traveled to Mexico and took a cruise with friends from Germany. The variety seemed to help me, at least, and with others driving and planning activities, all went very well. On the drive home from Florida disorientation occurred about four times, I drove most of the way. Next year we will be flying as we purchased a car to stay there. I am pleased with that, as the drive was stressful for me. One cannot disagree with him so I just have to let all things ride. I have maintained friendships much to his distress. He said I was becoming far too independent. He now sleeps more than before and forgetting names and misnaming people we have known for some time and it takes me awhile to catch on to whom he is referring. He seems disorganized with his garden and says he doesn't know what to put in anymore. I will wait and see how that goes. I find he is leaving clothes around the house much more than he used to. To-day he said we had spaghetti twice this week and we haven't had it at all. I am pleased that he sleeps well, that is a blessing.

May 2008 ♥

Things are going well, the garden will help and it seems when there is a routine, all is well. For a few weeks all will go well, one would almost forget there was a monster looming.

September 2008 ♥

The summer has been a repetition of many things, repeated stories, repeated angry outbursts and more threats of suicide He seems to crave sympathy as he finds many things wrong with his health. We make appointments with the doctor and while in the office he forgets what he was so upset about. He was worried about a sore knuckle in his right hand, scratchy throat, sore knee, sore hips, ringing of the ears hearing loss and recurring headaches once again. He has had the knee and hips x-rayed, an MRI of his head, hearing evaluation and will have his throat scoped in two weeks. He does have some arthritis showing up in his joints which is new to him, the MRI was clear and a hearing loss was confirmed. He received "over the ear" aids and didn't like the look of them so is requesting "in the ear replacements." I go with him to all appointments to hear what is said and to keep him on track. He loves to joke with the doctors and says everything is fine while he is there after an episode at home, in which he feels each issue is life threatening. I don't mean to make light of his fears, they are so important to him at home, and when at the doctor's office, are almost forgotten and I feel we have wasted the valuable time of the medical profession. If I try to make light of them to him at home, he accuses me of not caring.

My friend Beth spent two nights here as she is choosing her pup from Amy's litter of spaniels. She is quite a talker and John didn't like having to listen to her and he felt she took up too much of my time. We went to Amy's at 11 am, out to lunch around the mall, developed some pictures and back home by 5 pm. After she left, he lit into me. This "chewing out" went on and on and on. He belittled me as only he can do.

He says we never do things together so I suggested that he and I go to see "The Sound of Music". I asked him three times and each time he said no, and if I really wanted to go I should ask Mary. After our movie night, while at their house I brought up the idea to her and she said she would love to. As we were leaving the house, I mentioned to Bert and John that she and I would be planning our theater outing. Mary said perhaps Bert might like to go. Saying that in front of John confused him and he was immediately quiet. I said I would get back to them and we left. When we got into the car to come home, John lit into me saying I had no business bringing up such a surprise, without discussing it with him. He was adamant that I hadn't talked it over with him at all. This episode involved a lot of shouting and pouting, with many repetitions of the same angry accusations. I felt dead inside.

That incident led up to a major blow up two days later. He was angry that I go to yoga, have breakfasts with my friends twice a month and have luncheons with the retired teachers once a month. He said I was playing the Queen bee since we are "well off". Perhaps I was wrong in my retaliation, but I had reached my limit of the negativity. I said he could have every cent and that I would be fine living on my own, at least then I wouldn't be told off and would have peace. That seemed to register and he has been friendly for a day and a half. I am holding my breath.

It is a shame that the cup is always half empty. I try to cheer him up, even if I really don't feel that way myself. If I pretend to be happy, it does make me happy, and I try to see the best of the situation. Life is really a matter of attitude, I think.

Symptoms have recurred, thinking stores we drive by, are new, thinking that the Sporting Goods store is not where it was, and perceptions that we are driving in the wrong direction. I am thankful for one thing in that he wants me to drive pretty well all the time. I am not implying it is a peaceful drive, as I am instructed about each turn I should make, how I should slow down and how horrible all the other drivers are, on the road.

This writing is really therapeutic............life goes on..........

October 30, 2008 ♥

To-day we got talking about chelation therapy which Harold, age 90, participates in, and Eva and Luke are starting their sessions recently. I explained to John that since CT scans and MRI scans haven't showed any cause for headaches, perhaps it is a blood issue. We plan to try chelation in the spring. His fogginess continues and headaches as well as agitation, which springs up for no reason. We went out shopping and for lunch to-day, having things to do, help him pass the time, in better spirits.

To-day he is going to purchase the juice for his wine and admitted he didn't know how to calculate the cost of 72 liters at $2.50 per liter. I had found him stewing over the figures a few days before and he just pushed them aside and told me to be sure we had enough money on hand for the juice. This time he said" I can't remember how to do this."

We also installed the new kitchen taps and needed new shut off valves under the sink. He took some from other taps put them under the sink and said everything fit fine, while not using the new ones we had just bought. He spends a lot of time looking for things. He has misplaced a saw and is accusing Rodney of taking it on him. I know Rod hasn't borrowed any tools, so I must be more vigilant about his tools, I suppose. The only thing that is difficult is the anger he expresses against others, when he can't find what he wants.

He is worried when I am not around and gets very angry if I am out, saying I don't care for him and berating whomever I was with. (visit with Eva, the book club or yoga) I am determined to maintain some outside life not just for my own mental health, but also, so he can have some separation from me, as well.

I feel too much dependence would be unhealthy for both of us, in the long run. I must research this aspect of Alzheimer's and will follow whatever is suggested.

My doctor thought I should contact the Alzheimer's society for support. I am tempted. However one more thing requiring me to be away from home will be problematic.

November 2008 ♥

Forgetting where things are such as the tea pot, the kettle, the tea bags, where the wine glasses are, these are all routine happenings. We have added Amy's name to the title of the house, and cottage as it may become an issue, if the memory slips further and John's driving remains such a threat to our safety. It is an estate plan and a result of my fear of his driving. I feel he is going to kill us both someday. Better that it is taken care of now. (Advice: that was a big mistake. My trust was far too broad.)

Daily repetitions of routines, what day it is, what we want to do, where we have to go, continue. Each day I review the plan for the day and then repeat it a number of times as he gets stressed out if I "spring things on him". He gets very angry then, in spite of the fact I may have mentioned the topic the previous day.

I am researching Chelation therapy it looks good and will try to get it planned for when we are in Florida. It is naturopathy, I believe, so isn't covered no matter where you have it.

November 2008 – May 2009 ♥

Our winter south was routine. Jonathan seldom visited and we kept busy puttering around the apartments and golfing twice a week. We did enjoy bicycling around the neighborhood. Thankfully it is quiet and we had a regular route that was easy to follow. Repeating, angry outbursts, tearful regrets are becoming normal fare. Every day is very different. Fortunately books, movies and sleeping late have helped. I was able to persuade him to regular coffee trips to Panera and lunch at Golden Corral, both good outings which he enjoyed.

May 2009 ♥

We have gone to chelation therapy and found that his iron levels were toxic as well as aluminum, cadmium, and mercury. His homocysteine levels were in a dangerous range. Giving blood and folic acid pills, plus a regiment of vitamins are now a part of our routine. All my levels were normal. Chelation therapy was intended to clean toxic levels of mercury and lead from the blood streams of veterans after WW II. A liquid is taken intravenously that supposedly captures the metals and they are urinated out of the system. I suppose I am grasping for straws, hopefully it will help and delay the progress of the disease somewhat. I think this is called "bargaining" within the stages of grieving. (Denial, Anger, Bargaining, Depression, Acceptance)

We planted the garden to-day and he found it hard to get organized. He became anxious so we just took it slowly step by step, with my leading him. He says he will not have a garden next year as it doesn't interest him anymore. Leadership, once his strength is not there.

This is major. I have noticed he has forgotten how to program our thermostat and so that is another task I have taken over. He is sad much of the time and says he feels helpless, wishing the end to be near. He sleeps a lot, more than ever before. He seldom knows what day it is and asks me frequently what we have to do that day. He gets angry with me less often and is more compliant. When he makes a point that is in error, I let it go and move on to other things. He becomes anxious if I am away from him for any length of time. Previously, after 15 minutes away, he would say "you have been gone one hour" now he says "you don't care so you aren't here very much." The time element is lost. Logic is also lost. Planning and executing a project isn't possible. When he can't find something, he always wants to know what I did, with the item in question. We usually find what he wanted in a strange location. I have to become more vigilant about tools and when I see something out of place I replace it to its designated spot as soon as possible. Being meticulous about his tools was important to him previously and now that is disappearing.

He can't tolerate young people and is very critical of them so I try to keep a distance between he and the children for fear he will get angry with them without cause. Routine is very important. I am so thankful for Bert and Mary, as we go out every Tuesday to the show and Bert stays with him so I get an evening out. One really needs friends at such a time. Some are afraid and stay away.

It is interesting to see the different reactions to the knowledge of this disease. He constantly repeats himself and complains about the weather. This behavior has resulted in no one wanting to golf with him. We go ourselves three times a week for nine holes and it is exercise and a relaxed pace which is what he needs. With his knee surgery this week we will have to find something else to pass the time.

Still no contact with Jonathan, that doesn't help either. Amy just talks about Elsie, Rod's x, all the time, no help there either. She found his constant talking irritating when we drove north with them.

Saying to me, "How do you stand it?" She has absolutely no concept of what is happening and seems not to want to help at all. I have been left alone on this journey. I tried to share some of my feelings with her but she is very concerned only with her own life and the drama in it, so I just let her talk and take a deep breath.

He is reluctant to eat very much. It seems however when I put food in front of him he will eat it. It is just when asked what he would like he always says "nothing, I am not hungry." Whatever I make isn't good enough. There is a sadness around him that is difficult to lift. I try to ignore those times and change the subject so attention goes in another direction. Each day is a challenge.

May 18 2009 ♥

Yesterday was a difficult day. He was very depressed and angry. To-day he is the opposite. It is a roller coaster ride. He continues to forget what day it is and yesterday I counted how many times he repeated a story. The number of times was 8. I am trying very hard to be patient. His negativism does get me down and I find if I can escape for half an hour to the store, it helps me a great deal. I can pick up my spirits and start again.

May 28, 2009 ♥

He has forgotten how to use the telephone and the answering machine and in an attempt to hear messages pushed all the buttons and erased the welcome response. It is not too good as I would frequently call him if I was going to be late home or just to check in with him. He was happy when it rained and I stayed home from golf. We will be golfing together from now on as no one wants to be his partner since he is so negative and repeats the same stories over and over. I had told Jake about the situation, but now he has moved to a different course, so that partner is gone. One thing is better; his headaches are not as severe as previously. I don't know if that is significant.

June 2009 ♥

More confusion when I returned home to-day after golf. He asked me how I was going to get to the next town, on a bicycle and be able to do all that stuff. I said I would go later and left it at that. Don't quite know how to respond. The topic came out of the blue, since I had no need to go anywhere.

July 2009 ♥

The last few days have been better; he seems to have become more compliant. He still repeats himself, doesn't recognize familiar streets we are on and misnames things. The one new thing is that he was paranoid that the boys would wreck his outboard motor and therefore didn't let Amy and Rod take it north. We didn't go with them, as I knew it would be a disaster. He feels they are trying to take over the cottage since they never ask anymore, just announce that they are going. He has decided young people are lazy and up to no good, all of them. Kind of a grumpy old man……….. Such is life. We have been golfing several times and he likes that.

I think I have made a decision, when the time comes that he doesn't recognize me, that is when residential placement will be utilized. I will try to keep the memories alive for as long as possible. One feels guilty thinking that way. However I feel there will come a time, when I will be unable to manage his behaviors.

Yesterday was a very difficult one, he was angry about everything. I am trying to not take it personal but it is so hard. I have decided to take time with friends in spite of what he says or how he attempts to make me feel guilty. I need time for myself. My blood pressure is not the best and my health is perhaps also on the line………

August 2009 ♥

He had the air on with the windows open, didn't know it was August thinking it was May and on the way home from up north, challenged every highway I took, thinking I was going the wrong way. His put downs and arguments are more frequent and are repeated so many times. We had the German music in the car and that seemed to lift his spirits for a while. One day at a time……….To-day he forgot that he had had lunch and when I offered him ice cream, he said he had had it already. Fortunately he enjoys the garden and that keeps him busy. He doesn't want to join the golf club again next year and we will likely go back to the old club. No one wants to golf with him. He has the reputation there of being a complainer, which he is, unfortunately. The chelation therapy seems to have done some good as far as the numbers are concerned. His iron levels are almost normal. I don't know if it will slow the memory loss or even reverse it. Perhaps I am being too optimistic. He is ok as long as I am here with him……….I just can't go anywhere for any length of time. He doesn't want me golfing with the ladies now and he tries to make me feel guilty when I "leave him all alone".

On Monday we went over to the old golf course to see about the 2010 memberships and Bruce was there. In conversation John had forgotten that the course had 18 holes and that Bruce would remember that we had played there before. To-day is Wednesday and he forgot what day it was and asked what month we were in, thinking it was September already.

He forgot we had a fertilizer spreader and I reminded him that it was in the garden shed and that we had brought it up from Florida the last time we drove. He was anxious again to-day about me golfing with the women to-morrow. I assured him I would cancel my tee time and would try a different golf course with him to-morrow. Since we will be leaving the new course anyway, one missed day won't make any difference, I suppose. I may call the Alzheimer's society to find out the correct manner for handling anxious behavior.

Sept. 2009 ♥

Anxiety and paranoia are symptoms of Alzheimer's and they have both started. Lunch with Eva and Janice led to his tears, threats of suicide and not speaking to me for several hours. He says I don't care about him or I wouldn't run off, "all the time"-One lunch in two months. It is hard to separate the person from the behavior. I realize the disease is playing a big part, however when you are the brunt of the attack, it isn't pleasant.

To-day I had an appointment with Dr. Jackson, was going to drop off clothes at the shelter, go to the bank. Get gas, get Metamucil and to buy beer. I was gone two hours, the performance when I returned was amazing, I had told him all the things I had to do, and he forgot all of them and thought I had gone to see Suzanne. I haven't seen her in quite a number of weeks. I must go out there soon. She has Alzheimer's and it is a joy to visit her, as she is so happy. I really don't understand the disease. ……..

This week has been eventful. I reminded John that I had an appointment with Dr. Jackson on three occasions, he forgot and was angry when I came home, thinking I had been to the next town to buy gas. We never buy gas there.

After a nice dinner at golf, sitting across from Harvey and Eve, he said, on the way home, "I wonder why Harvey and Eve weren't there.

Driving home from the diner, after breakfast, the next day, he commented on a green light that was on the left side of an intersection saying "I guess people might think they can drive down that way" "that way" being toward oncoming traffic.

I am encouraging him to express himself, as it is a window into where his thoughts are taking him. The repetitions are what get me down and the anger that is associated with several topics.

October 2009 ♥

Golfing has helped tremendously, the exercise and fresh air help keep me sane. John forgets his score and where his ball is however I don't make a deal about it and we seldom keep score now. We gave some money to Rod and Amy, at first he thought it was $600 then $50,000 then $500,000 quite a range, at least he had the joy of understanding that it was a gift and it made him happy. He has told me about 6 times already that Carl next door, who is dying of cancer, is now bedridden. I am pleased that he hasn't spoken of dying lately since he is back on the trazodone. He has refused to take all the pills that Dr. Jackson has prescribed. I am not going to fight with him every day. Peace is far more important. He was beginning to say I was trying to kill him with all the pills. Now he is on the bare minimum.

The remote on the television confuses him so I wrote out all the channels he is likely to watch so now he can find them. At times he presses the wrong button and swears at the television as if it is the television's fault. He forgets which button to push. To-day he said, "Sometimes I wake up and don't know where I am" and "I feel like I don't belong here and don't know what to do". "I feel I should be somewhere else". That was a clear window into how it is for him. No wonder he is afraid.

I tell him not to worry, as it is likely his cold and that he will feel better to-morrow.

Oct 30 2009 ♥

    I am still struggling with whether or not to tell him his diagnosis, I tend to feel it would defeat him, so life goes on. On Monday, he said it again, "Sometimes I don't know where I am or if I belong here" On Wednesday he forgot what Rod's job was and asked Amy what he did at the shop. His headaches still persist.

    He has refused to take all the meds that Dr. Jackson had recommended, saying I was trying to poison him, so I have stopped them and will introduce them back gradually. He also didn't want to return for chelation, feeling it was a money grab. I felt it did reduce the headaches to a degree, so I am undecided. Every day he forgets what day it is and asks what month it is. I am looking forward to Florida as it will keep him more active and will be a diversion. He has started to doubt Bert's friendship and this is very hard. It started when he was confused by the programmable thermostat and felt lost when he tried to explain it to him. He was confused more than ever. That somehow became Bert's fault….. He has turned down three dinner invitations, due to this issue.

    We went walking on a day when John was particularly negative. I decided to count all the negative issues he brought up. In a 45 minute walk, he had 29 complaints. That day I was able to shut most of it out. His headaches and light headedness persist. I don't know what it means. He is on the lipitor so hopefully he will not suffer a stroke as his Mom did.

    I try to remain positive. Fortunately I look forward to lunch with the girls on Wednesday this week, so that will be nice.

Lora Kristoff

Nov. 2009 ♥

Time in Florida was good and bad. We had a regular routine, breakfast on the patio then a bike ride or a drive down to the beach. He lets me drive so that helps with my anxiety with his driving skills (slipping fast). I try to arrange one activity each day so we have something to look forward to. I find I must repeat over and over whatever is scheduled so he is reassured what the plan is. He gets upset that we don't see Jonathan very often even with them living so close. He still has issues with Anna and cannot keep them to himself. We were invited by our mailman to attend a fish fry at his church on Friday evening and he agreed. It was quite a drive up Dixie Highway and he became anxious looking for street numbers. When we found it he had a complete panic attack in the parking lot and wouldn't go in for dinner. We then drove to a familiar spot, a local restaurant and had a quiet dinner, just the two of us. It is becoming harder and harder to go out anywhere. That was the first full blown panic attack.

Dec 2009 ♥

Jonathan and Anthony came over, by themselves, for Christmas. Anna doesn't come anymore. They are having some difficulties that I don't want to be involved in. They are adults and can sort things out, I am sure. I have enough on my plate. Golfing is a nice distraction, however we don't keep score anymore and John has to be reminded where to drive to the next tee off. Disorientation is becoming the norm. It is hard for me since previously, I never had to pay attention to such things and now more details are left to me. I have noticed he is less and less interested in any repairs around the property and so I must find someone to do little chores for us that he always took care of in the past. He spends a great deal of time in the shed sorting things, although order never seems to be the result of his time spent.

January 2010 ♥

He continues to be afraid of the strangest things and double checks the locks on the doors, thinking someone will be coming in during the night. He has a large stick beside the door and beside the bed. When I asked what they were for he said, "For when someone breaks in." From my reading I know paranoia is part of the disease and it is becoming more evident for us now. I want to discuss it with Dr. Bernard when we get home in the event a change of medications might be in order for him to relieve the worry from his mind.

February 2010 ♥

He is very depressed and has been talking suicide, which scares me. I remind him of all he has to be thankful for, and nothing seems to cheer him up. I finally persuaded him to plan a trip to Europe. I know there is a big reunion planned for 2011 when the class will celebrate being 75. I don't think we can wait another year before returning one more time. I know it will likely be our last trip to Europe and I want him to be able to have that enjoyment, one more time. The disease is making him very difficult. One doesn't know, is it the disease or side effects of medications, or parts of his personality, just being expressed with no inhibition?

He has been very critical of Amy and Rod, not just Jonathan. I have been able to keep a lid on it so far, as I don't want more alienation or there will be no family left, when all is said and done. I realize his parents were critical of many, so perhaps it is just a coping mechanism that is "hard wired". Still it is not easy to live with, balancing everyone's feelings and trying to keep the waters as calm as possible. No wonder my blood pressure is rising.

March 2010 ♥

We had a nice birthday celebration, a quiet lunch out with Victor. Quiet perhaps isn't the word to be used as Victor never stops talking. He was kind enough to drive and that was a nice change. I always sit in the back of his big car since he is a terrible driver and I feel that is likely the safest place to be. John was relaxed with him as there were no demands on talking and food was the order of the day. Jonathan didn't appear for his father's birthday. Perhaps I will invite he and Tony for a steak dinner. That usually works.

April 2010 ♥

Time to return north, John has asked Gordon, a tenant, to watch over things while we are away. He is good at repairs, electrical, plumbing etc. and we arranged a reduction in rent to allow for his time. He seemed pleased with the agreement. I am relieved since John shies away from any repair.

May 2010 ♥

We had a fairly good time in Florida without too many incidents apart from the one big one, when John told Jonathan to "go to hell". That really put a damper on the time there. Since that time, he has said the same thing to me, on more than one occasion, however it doesn't have the same impact since now, I kind of expect it whenever

I dare to disagree with him. The words cut to your soul, I know it is the disease talking, but knowing that doesn't take away the pain. The anger is more frequent and more intense and the confusion is evident in almost all of the conversation. That is the reason why we are heading to Europe on May 27. Hopefully he can have some quality time with his cousin and his wife, and with our friends' help, it might be accomplished, in that loving environment.

I have found that he cannot plan any activity such as planting the garden or packing clothes. He gets upset easily if I try to have any time to myself. He is losing words more frequently and watches the same program without being aware he watched it already. Repeating himself is ongoing and my patience is wearing very thin. The anger is the worst part, whatever I say or do, there is always an issue.

July 2010 ♥

Our trip to Europe was great. It was nice to visit everyone one last time. John was confused on the plane thinking it was a ship and vowed to go home by train instead. I'm sure others noticed the changes, however they were very kind. It is easy to blend with a group and listen to their stories rather than ours. When we arrived back home, we went to the doctor and he gave him a memory test and has pulled his driver's license and told him, "John you have Alzheimer's." I don't think it registered as he just said, "I have a sore knee".

Life is having its ups and downs, I contacted the Alzheimer's society and they have sent me some information. There are 100 clients to one counselor, so their contact will be limited. I have followed some of their suggestions, leaving notes, reminding him of the day and what we have planned for that day. I am now working on removing clutter and organizing my life in the event something happens to me. He is paranoid about my time and my intentions. He still gets angry about my show night with Mary on Tuesdays, saying that I don't love him if I insist on going out. Bert comes over so they have time together. Having friends that understand is most important. Their patience is invaluable.

The counselor from the Geriatric unit at the hospital is coming over on Wednesday morning. They offered their support and I am going accept any help that comes our way. Dr. Bernard says I am not to leave him alone, however he doesn't want to come with me shopping, so I try to make all my trips short ones and leave a note saying when I will return. So far that is working.

October 2010 ♥

Things are gradually progressing if you can call it that. John is more confused and more anxious whenever I go out. I try to leave for a little while each day so he is assured I am coming back when I have a longer errand from time to time. He rarely wants to leave the house and is perfectly happy as long as we are sitting together. He said to me that at times he doesn't know where he is. It must be a frightening experience. We try to do one project each day so he has something to think about. He seems to have a slight cold as he has chills and he gets sweaty whenever he does a little activity. We have stopped golfing for the season and we are both looking forward to heading south.

November 2010 ♥

Florida proved to be stressful since Jonathan avoided us. I can't really blame him. Of course, Anna never comes so that is another topic of negativity that he repeats and repeats. He is unable to do any repairs and just walks away whenever a problem arises. We are fortunate to have a list of competent people for repairs. Golfing doesn't hold any interest for him and he just wants to sit and watch television.

He still spends a lot of time in the shed sorting things, however when I go and see what he is doing, things are all over the place.

He has started berating Anthony, our grandson, and that is not fair or just. He projects his negativity from Jonathan to his son.

It is really hard to watch and hard to tolerate, changing his position can't be done. It is just as well they seldom come. It is not fair to Anthony. I thought watching his hockey would cheer him up, not so…..this disease is not kind at all. I try to shield both Jonathan and Tony, as much as I can, as I can read when an episode is about to emerge.

I am always on egg shells.

He has started hoarding things and has many things he collects and handles over and over again.

The research says this is normal.

Feb 2011 ♥

He threatened to kill me in front of Victor and Gordon. A frond had dropped from the large palm tree and the three of them were cutting it up in pieces to go into the dumpster. While he had the butcher knife in his hand he made the motion to his neck and said "this is what will happen to you, if you don't behave"…..I was so embarrassed and hurt. It is one thing to speak threats in private and quite another to have them said out loud in the company of others. I went into the apartment and cried my eyes out…. Then out, with a smile and refreshments for everyone. I don't know how much I can take of this…

I have asked Jonathan to come and spend time in the afternoons, for two hours, so I can go to the movies to escape. He is unemployed and time together may mend fences, I hope.

I know it isn't easy for him to spend time with his father. I try to entice him with a steak dinner and cheesecake.

One morning while making the bed, I noticed a butcher knife on his side table. When I asked him what it was doing there, he said, "in case someone comes in at night." I took a picture of it…..unbelievable and very scary.

The next time he threatened to kill me, he gave me a choice, cut my throat, shoot me, or drowning. I was to take my pick. The research tells me this is not a good sign. I am really starting to get frightened.

March 2011 ♥

We returned north and he was upset that it was cold and wanted immediately to return south. We flew down after two weeks at home, having dropped off our tax information to our accountant, and stayed in Florida until the beginning of June. It had been a cool spring so it was better for him to be able to get out in the sunshine, down south. While we were there, he had an episode, we went bike riding and he became dizzy and lay down by the sidewalk. I was in a panic since I thought perhaps he had had a stroke. He was extremely pale and couldn't stand. I left him there and raced home on my bike hoping that Victor would be there and could come with his big car and pick him up. Only Gordon was home and he helped me get him home, his bike and myself.

He went to bed and slept two hours. I knew it was time to return to home and booked our flights that day.

We arrived at the airport and Rod and Amy picked us up and drove us to an Italian restaurant, near the airport. While driving there, he announced to them that he is going to kill me. Amy looks at me and says to him, "Don't talk like that." She has no idea…..I have to get him more help and help for myself, I feel I cannot go on much longer and keep my sanity. I have been getting tightness in my chest....

June 2011 ♥

I made an appointment with Dr. Bernard for him and Dr. Jones for myself. I wrote a letter, in advance, to Dr. Bernard outlining all the things that he was doing and saying, in order that he would have a clear picture and could give me more guidance. This disease is really starting to scare me.

Dr. Bernard was very clear on the next steps, he will need residential care. It is just a matter of when and where. He instructed me to contact the Alzheimer's society, get a counsellor, and contact CCAC for the procedures for residential care. He says there is usually a 6 month waiting period. Therefore it is important that I start immediately.

He also was imperative that if he threatens to kill me one more time, I am to call 911, he made me promise.

Two days passed before the next threat came. It was a Sunday night. I told John I had to call 911. He begged me not to call and promised he would go with me to Emergency the next day. I agreed and he went.

He was admitted to the Psychiatric Wing for observation and to modify the medications for depression and paranoia. Amy and Rod seem to realize there is something wrong now. They don't say much so I will just follow all the advice of the professionals. One must have a clear head with such big decisions. I know the doctors deal with these situations often, so they know what is needed better than I.

Amy and I went to see the counselor at the Alzheimer's society. I had a surprise in that, Amy agreed with everything the counselor said and added more information about her father's strange behaviors. She just laughed about it as if it was perfectly normal, saying, "That is just the way he is." The counselor did try to inform her that threats of suicide and murder are definitely not normal. Amy didn't want to listen. <u>I think I am now completely alone.</u>

While John was in the hospital, I could get all the appointments done and visited some homes, to make a choice.

There are so many. I have to choose 6 and list them in order of priority. I want private, near home, accessible for Amy, so she can visit. The home also has to be one that I would feel comfortable living in myself.

I think I can hold on until November.

Dr. Jones has given me a warning about my blood pressure. She has put me on another pill. She has made an appointment with Dr. Melford, the heart doctor. She says I am in stroke territory and I must, must take this very seriously. She said "If you have a stroke you can't help him at all."

I made the excuse that I get up too many times at night and he needs a restful night, so I am sleeping alone in the bedroom upstairs. He is angry about that as well. He didn't like the downstairs bedroom saying it was a dungeon, so we switched. That works much better since the floors squeak, and hearing whenever he gets up, I can prepare and try to redirect him each time.

I know I haven't been able to sleep properly for some time and lately have been putting a chair behind the door so I will hear him if he comes in the room. The butcher knife on the side table in the bedroom, in Florida, frightened me completely. I must put a lock on the bedroom door so I get a bit of sleep at least. The doctor says that he is being controlled by the disease and he will do whatever the disease tells him to do. I am afraid of his rages. It is hard to understand that a person that looks so normal would be capable of changing so much. I don't know where the man I married is.

July 2011 ♥

I figured out how to put the bathroom locks on the bedroom door. I made that exchange without too much difficulty. John has to be watched all the time. He wanted to take apart the gas fireplace thinking the pilot light gave off too much heat….I came home from grocery shopping to find him with parts all over the family room floor. I quickly called Bert and he came over and turned off the gas line valve further back so that is taken care of. Next he thought the same thing about the gas water heater in the basement and he shut off the pilot. I tried to explain to him that we need hot water. There is no logic, so my words were to no avail. In attempts to re-light the pilot, there was an explosion and he burned the hair on his hands. I know now this is getting dangerous.

I got to the heart doctor and she says I have a leaky mitral valve that is caused by high blood pressure. I have to consider my health and ability to take care of John. Amy is no help at all and Jonathan just hides.

He has lost his sense of time so day and night are interchangeable. The lack of sleep is killing me.

There are two good choices of residence, The Pines or The Grove. They are both run by the same company. The Pines would be easy for Amy to reach from her home.

I try to walk for about 20 minutes each day around the neighborhood. It gives me some peace and relief from the rages and criticism.

Florida is being taken care of now by Gordon, he and his girlfriend have split up, don't know the details.

He has moved into our empty unit until he finds something for himself. At least I don't have to worry about that as well. I enrolled John in the Day Program for adults at The Grove. He goes Monday, Wednesday and Friday.

It is designed to give respite for caregivers and I tend to sleep while he is gone. I am exhausted.

They are very positive there and Steven, his close friend, is also going. That has helped.

The threats of murder and suicide continue, he has now said it in front of Steven and Betty, Andrew and June, Jonathan and Tony, Amy and Rod, Victor and Gordon, as well as, Kenneth at the day program. He says it many times, when we are on our own and each time it cuts to the core.

I have started going to the Alzheimer's society meetings once a week. After supper John tends to fall asleep and I am only gone for one hour and a half. Sometimes Luke comes over and keeps him company. Both he and Eva have been wonderful giving me support. I think people in our generation realize far more than the younger ones. The little things mean so much.

There is a library at the Alzheimer's society and I have been devouring the books on care, residence expectations, therapy, emotional needs, fears, medications and supports. There is so much to learn. I have also inquired into the geriatric program at the College and may enroll in a course on dementia. I want to take the proper steps for his care, both now and in the future. I need to prepare myself for what is ahead as well.

I purchased a book for Jonathan and Amy, "The 36 hour Day" by Mace and Rabins. It was highly recommended for family education.

Hope they read it. It would be nice if I could share this journey with them.

I can't count the number of nights I cried and cried. If John saw my tears, then he would apologize and would be decent for a day or so, then back to the criticism and belittling. That never ended no matter what I did or said. I just tried to escape in novels, watching television in the living room or on the computer. All those things also made him angry. I have nowhere to turn. Alzheimer's is a cruel disease.

Lack of sleep was the worst, as he would wander throughout the night and also get angry at me and wake me to tell me off about some minor item. Then he would finally fall asleep and I could not.

Aug 2011 ♥

I received the call Friday Aug 12 at 10:30 am. There is a private room available at The Grove and he is to be admitted on Monday. If I turn it down, he goes to the bottom of the list and the time line is unknown.

The Grove was my first choice of the six, and a private room, so I can't turn it down as it is a wonderful location.

I have to purchase furniture and gather all the things they ask for, to set up his room.

I called Amy and told her I need her help moving furniture and that everything will be in Bert's garage on Saturday afternoon. I quickly went to Costco, bought a dresser and a television and then Bert and his son came over and picked up chairs from the family room. All was over at Bert's before John came home at 4pm from the day program. Fortunately Amy and Rod and Bert and Louis moved everything for me on Saturday so the room would be ready for him on Monday. I moved an old chair in the place of his leather one and when he came home, he didn't even notice the change.

We had a quiet weekend together. I just agreed with whatever he said.

Monday, Aug 15 2011 ♥

The move went rather well. I told him he needed to be there so the doctors and nurses could watch over him and that I would always come to visit him. He liked the room and said, "This is a nice place."

I was so relieved.

Apparently Amy just cried, when they moved things in, according to Bert. She has no idea what this disease is.

Jonathan came north looking for work. I was able to set him up with our accountant. He found a position for him with a church organization. He is desperate for work. He stayed with Amy and Rod, while he was here.

He seems neutral about his father. Little is said, as always. I know he has suffered the criticism and it has left many scars on him and in him. I hope he will be able to carry on. I think he is the only one that will understand what I am living now and have been for some time. He shuts people out and hides, that is his way of coping.

The criticism does cut deep. I would go to bed crying many nights, vowing that I would try harder to-morrow.

Sept 2011 ♥

I asked Jonathan, Amy and Rod, to come over as I wanted to talk over the whole situation. I prepared a letter outlining the past years' experiences, hoping they would receive the decisions made, with some understanding.

Well the ---- hit the fan as the saying goes. I was attacked by Amy and Rod, while Jonathan, looked on.

All accuse me of many things. It seemed they came with a set agenda and were prepared for a fight. Listening and understanding were not the order of the day. I had hoped for understanding and support and instead I was attacked. They feel I should not have "Put him in a home" and that now I am "living high". I was dumbfounded. All I want is to be left alone and finally have some peace. It was a blur of angry words. I know I called Rod a bully, with his demands. They are free to say whatever they want and believe whatever they want.

They certainly don't understand and were completely unwilling to listen to what I had to say. Their anger was breathtaking. I didn't have the energy for the fight so I will just let them rattle on. I was thankful when they finally left. Now I am completely alone.

I know I am doing what is best for John and I will never abandon him. He told me what to do for these last few years, now they are trying to step into his shoes and continue the pattern. Better to be alone, than live with more criticism. John warned me that Amy and Rod were "taking over" perhaps he was right. I always gave them the benefit of the doubt.

The Alzheimer's society say that the disease breaks up families and that is exactly what is happening.

I didn't give him the disease and I can't fix it. If only they had educated themselves, such a shame.

Jonathan only stayed, I think two weeks, then walked away from his contract and returned to a job in Florida.

I have apologized to our accountant, many times for his behavior.

I cannot rush them through their stages of grief and they are certainly stuck in the "Denial and Anger Stages" and likely will be for some time. Psychologically, people enjoy anger. It gives them an emotion they can easily relate too. It takes far less understanding and effort and is based in fear.

The family will have to travel their own stages of grief as I am. It hurts not to have their support. I have enough to carry right now and will focus my energy on my husband. He is the one in need of care and attention.

Oct 2011 ♥

Amy arrived when I was at the residence and she was ready to fight, once again. I tried to avoid her since it would only upset John and stress isn't good for him. She followed me out to the car, after I had told him, they could visit and I would return after she had gone. She started on about how this was affecting her. Unfortunately, I couldn't restrain myself and told her that the Alzheimer's wasn't all about her and she must consider her father's needs. I left and two hours later, returned and calmed him down and we had a relaxing evening. I stayed for supper and had a quiet evening with him. It then turns into how we spent our evenings at home, watching the news and talking from time to time.

Nov 2011 ♥

Amy and Rod want to challenge my POA. They met with the administrator, and she showed them all the papers and they saw that they are next in line to care for him, if I cannot. They wanted to know the procedures to challenge me and she told them that the Provincial Trustee could overthrow a POA, if it was deemed I was not diligent in my duty. She also told them that she would review the care I was giving and meet with them again.

She completed her review and met with them and said that her only role would be to provide a report to the Trustee and that if asked, her report would indicate that I was not only fulfilling my duty, but was going above and beyond what was expected or required and that that would be her report, if one was requested.

I have been invited on a small trip with the book club ladies for one week. I feel I really need to get away, however I feel I shouldn't be away from John for too long. I have decided to go and will book visits for John each day, with others, while I am gone, so he is never alone. Sedona, Arizona. We rented a house, a huge house and had a wonderful time. I did a lot of crying and a lot of healing during that week and it was good for me. Good friends are so precious.

I am planning a major renovation of our kitchen. I have a great deal of nervous energy that has to be dealt with. I am also in the process of painting all the rooms in the house. They have not been painted in 35 years. Brian and Bert have helped with all the renovations. It is so refreshing to have something else to occupy my mind. I really think that working is my therapy and it allows the pain to subside for many hours. I am so physically tired that I sleep really well. A night's sleep was very rare for me while he was at home. I know that very competent people are watching over him so his safety and my safety are taken care of.

Dec 2011 ♥

About midnight on December 2, I received a phone call from the Police telling me to stop harassing Amy. Rod doesn't want me to email her anymore. I had been providing updates to both she and her brother, regarding their father's experiences. I don't have a problem with no e mails. I told the officer that they were likely drunk and that I would co-operate fully. The next week I visited the police station to get a copy of the report and none had been filed. They considered it a non-incident.

Rod also left me quite a message on my answering machine, telling me that I needed psychiatric help and that he was concerned about John's freedom. I have had numerous hang up phone calls, day and night.

The one blessing is that when they are angry, they don't talk to you and that part I can certainly live with.

The holidays will be a challenge. I will leave a note for Amy, informing her that I will spend Christmas Eve with John and they can spend Christmas Day with him. I have been invited to spend Christmas with Bert and Mary. I really don't feel comfortable with that, intruding on their family gathering. I may take the bus north for a couple of days to stay with Marie, my sister.

I haven't spent a Christmas with my family in over 40 years.... That wasn't ever considered a possibility. That made me very sad on many occasions. I tried for Easter or Thanksgiving and that was not permitted either.

It is very different being able to decide things for myself.

I want John to feel safe since the Alzheimer's workshops said that fear, is their strongest emotion. I am going to try to find visiting companions, so he won't be alone too much.

I requested that he continue in the Day Program while a resident at The Grove, paying the extra for the participation in their daily activities, since I don't feel John will willingly participate otherwise. That option is not possible since he would be crossing programs and taking the spot of someone perhaps with greater need. I understand that so I decided to approach each of the research recommendations, to optimize stimulation.

I have summarized supports that the research say will be helpful in providing mental stimulation:

1. Set routines- Routines are set with meal and snack and recreational schedules.
2. Aroma Therapy-., lavender oil and lavender air fresheners for aroma.
3. Pet Therapy- Visiting service dogs provide some animal contact.
4. Music Therapy- I purchased a cd player and a dvd player and brought in about 60 cd's of German music which he really enjoys. I was able to borrow German dvd's from a gentleman

at the German Club. He downloads them from a German television station he receives. He is quite a technical wizard and a generous gentle soul. I pick up about 4 or 5 and return them each month exchanging them for a new set.

5. <u>Art Therapy</u>- Art therapy included assembling and painting model boats that I found at Michael's craft store. We also painted small bird houses from the Dollar Store. These activities seemed to calm him down and he eagerly sat with me at the card table in his room. We gifted all our birdhouses to various departments in the home along with Christmas sweets. He really enjoyed wrapping and delivering them to everyone.

6. <u>Exercise Therapy</u>- Exercise happens when we walk the mall or take a trip to the city park, sometimes we just walk the halls at the Grove. It is warm and level and he meets familiar faces along the way and he enjoys that.

7. <u>Laughter Therapy</u>- Laughter, I work very hard at concealing moments of sadness and loss that I feel while I am with him. I have to work at being cheerful sometimes with all that is going on. It is very important for him, I know since stress will only have a negative impact on his progress.

8. <u>Light Therapy</u>- I was able to find a light at Shoppers Drug Mart that has the correct lumens to reduce the effects of depression, usually associated with winter months. It looks quite modern and really brightens up his room.

9. <u>Socialization</u>- I have been so fortunate in finding a gentleman, Conrad, who is willing to be a day time companion for John. Conrad drives the bus for the day program so was available and appreciated the extra hours of activity between bus runs. It is wonderful. He takes John out to the coffee shop, attends church services, makes sure he is present for musical performances, and participates in Therapeutic touch etc. during the day.

10. <u>Life Review-</u>. I wrote a brief life story and read it to John frequently. He listens intently to it and smiles from time to

time. It is hard to know if it registers. It perhaps is something like the activity in "The Notebook" (a wonderful movie about Alzheimer's).
11. <u>Personal Memorabilia-</u> I filled his walls with family pictures, that he has started to talk to.
12. <u>Massage Therapy</u>- I hired Katie a beautiful redhead massage therapist to give him an in- house massage once a week.
13. <u>Problem Solving</u>- Problem solving and sorting were accomplished with jigsaw puzzles. We assembled them, pasted them on cardboard and displayed them around his room. He really enjoyed that activity for a fairly long period of time. Gradually one could observe lapses in ability so we stopped before it was too frustrating for him.
14. <u>Sorting Exercises</u>
15. <u>Field Trips</u>. I regularly take him out to various places: McDonald's for coffee and a muffin, walking around Wal-Mart, visiting Steven, his friend, drives to the city park to feed the birds, to the next town, to visit friends etc. I also accompany him on bus trips organized by the recreation department. I want him to get used to participating.

The Christmas season at the residence is festive. The staff decorated the areas very nicely. I have been practicing Christmas Carols and he seems to enjoy sitting and listening to them. My skill at playing the piano was brought down a peg or two when Mrs. Nelson came down to the area where the piano is and a staff member said to her. "You can enjoy the music." Her reply was, "I guess it is better than silence."

I had a wonderful visit with Marie and Anita, my sisters, for two days over Christmas. Gerry, Anita's husband, isn't doing so well, so his health is a concern for her.

She still enjoys working and it is good for her to have a time to herself.

Feb 2012 ♥

Amy and I avoid each other. There is no need for outbursts. She will understand sooner or later.

I was able to find people to work with John to help keep him mentally more alert. Conrad works with him during the day and Angela and Donna work with him at night. Katie gives him a full body massage once a week. All these things were recommended in the research. Hopefully the support will help him stay alert longer. It also provides me with time to rest, spend time with friends and renovate our home. I keep quite a schedule for him so that he is hardly ever alone. Amy's visits are infrequent. I let her know I would leave Wednesdays open for her or she could choose whatever dates that would work for her and I will accommodate her preferences. No response.

March 2012 ♥

I left a note for Amy, no emails allowed, informing her that I plan to rent the cottage and if she wants to use it, she can give me the dates and I will hold those dates open for her. She wrote on the bottom of my note.

"We won't be going to the cottage." That also is not a problem.

I have established a routine going to see John. I shower him each time since only two showers per week are on the schedule for residents and he always liked to shower daily in the past.

He is afraid they are stealing his clothes so I bring them home to wash and iron them. They tend not to bleach the undershirts so they are gray. He still wants his shirts white and ironed and a crease down the front of the pant leg. We usually go out for a drive, walk around at the mall, go to a local park and sometimes to the movies.

April 2012 ♥

John and I went to see our accountant, with the income tax papers. He recognized him but didn't know his name. His speech is getting more and more off topic and German words are increasing quite a bit.

I phoned Germany on my cell phone from his room and he told them we would come by to visit to-morrow. He didn't know what to say and handed me the phone to talk, giving up on having a conversation.

I have had to make several short 3 day trips to Florida, four messy evictions, new window installations, replacing the entire sewer system, new doors, painting both buildings and all the city permits that go along with each process. The units needed a great deal of updating since John had let things go for some time. I am glad that I have so many people hired to support him, whenever I am not there. I also get some reprieve.

May 2012 ♥

I got back to the heart doctor for a checkup and the news isn't good. I now have three valves that are leaking, the mitral, tricuspid and aortic. The measurement is 4.8 and Dr. Melford says they do surgery when it is at 5.2. I don't understand all the details, I had a hard time listening. She asked if I had any stress in my life……

Gerry, Anita's husband, died of diabetic complications. His organs just started to shut down. He had been on morphine for leg pain for quite some time and slept a great deal. Anita had a small gathering at the house with immediate family and it was really nice. She and the boys spread some of his ashes in the backyard, the remainder, he wanted put in the ocean in a bay near St John's, where he used to play as a child. Marie suggested that we, three sisters, take a trip to Newfoundland. I was put in charge of booking the reservations.

I will make it a very short trip, as I don't want to be away from John for too long. It is so nice that I am now able to give my sister support, when she needs it.

It was nice to get away for a while, upon my return he just said, "You weren't here yesterday." I said, "That is right, I couldn't make it." He said "OK" and that was it. He has no sense of time anymore. All the things the Alzheimer's course spoke about are now showing up. I am so glad I took that course, matter of fact, I went twice. The second time I learned much more and was able to ask more questions for our situation, while the first time I was just in a state of awe. They are very patient.

July - August 2012 ♥

We have a schedule now and John and I go on little trips every time I visit him. I like to take him out, so he gets a change of scene. We have been down to visit Steven. He is at the Pines, a residential facility. He needs a great deal of care, walking is limited and it seems like he will be wheelchair bound very soon.

Amy and Rod tend to upset John when they visit and there have been episodes of aggression, with him, after their visits. The residence called me one evening to come and calm him down. I have left notes for them to bring him laughter and joy, however they have their own agenda and they don't seem to see what they are doing to him. John now wears a wander bracelet as they fear he will walk out someday when someone else comes in. He can be very quick on his feet. I have asked the doctor to consider an alteration in his meds to reduce his anxiety. He gets very antsy with the sun downing and he can't sit still after supper even to watch the news. I hate to see him in such stress.

I attended the annual review and they went over all the things they track. They certainly have extensive records.

It is wonderful to know they are watching over him so completely. John thinks people are looking in the windows at night and he insists on closing the blinds in the sitting area. He now thinks that is his living room and he doesn't like anyone else to come there. He pinned another resident that has cerebral palsy, up against the wall because he came and sat in "his living room". It was one thing to have him aggressive toward me, quite another when it is against a stranger. The residence calls me on the phone whenever there is an episode.

They are becoming more frequent.

Sept 2012 ♥

I have been blessed with so many friends. The book club ladies meet once a month and plan excursions, the retired teachers every other Friday morning for breakfast and the golfing ladies every Saturday morning. I have been working on the renovation of the house. It hasn't been painted and needs to be updated. Brian has been wonderful, doing the work for me. It all helps me focus on other things and keeps me very busy. There is so much stuff to get rid of. I would sell a lot however I am nervous about strangers coming to the house so will store the big things for now.

Bert and Mary are fantastic. They have invited me to join them for dinner and dominoes. I went a few Wednesday evenings, however it is a couples' thing they do with Rita and Manfred, so I feel out of place.

Anita and Don, her son, and the girls have been down for a night at Great Wolf Lodge. I hadn't planned to join them, however was glad that I did. It was quite an experience.

I have a regular routine with John and have others with him when I am not there so he is well cared for and is doing far more now than he ever did while at home. I know I couldn't provide everything he has at the home.

October 2012 ♥

I received a call that they want to move him to the secure wing. He, looking quite normal, has tried to exit the building a few times. His aggressive behavior, after Amy's visits has resulted in episodes with other residents and staff. I cross referenced the dates and 6 of the 7 incidents occurred after she had visited. She just doesn't understand. She is hurting her father, showing her emotions and not bringing him laughter and happiness. His last memories of her are leaving a bad feeling for him. Jonathan hasn't been to see his father since last year in September 2011. I guess when the depression took over and John was unhappy and critical, no matter what anyone did. It is hard for Jonathan, to overlook that and recognize it, as part of the disease.

It is easy to consider it now, however when you live it day in and day out it is very, very hard….

November, 2012 ♥

An opportunity came up with Nancy and Melissa. Melissa turns 60 this year and planned to spend three weeks in Venice. They invited me to join them. I decided I would go for one week. They speak Italian and know the city. It is flood season so it should be interesting. The trip was fantastic, flew by and I had a wonderful time. When I returned to John, he said "You weren't here yesterday." I said, "No, I couldn't make it" and he said, "OK". I had arranged friendly visits for him every day while I was away with Conrad, Angela, Katie and Donna.

December 2012 ♥

Back into the routine, I am planning once again to go north to Marie and Anita's for the holiday. This time I will stop at Anita's and go with her up to Marie's on Christmas day. Kevin is coming from out west, so it will be nice to see him. The trip was great, Vicky and Don were also there and young children make Christmas special. I gave money gifts to the niece and nephews. Giving to them is something John wouldn't let me do for years. I am glad that I can do it once again.

January 2013 ♥

Time is flying by, John seems relaxed now, however I had to stop the massages as he refuses to take his clothes off for Katie. She has been great. Ruth hasn't worked out either, he just doesn't like her. I found another lady, Nancy, through Kenneth, at the residence. John seems to like her and she brings in her dog, so that is a nice change.

She may not last too long since she may be moving away. Angela and Conrad are tried and true. I can always depend on them it seems.

Feb - March 2013 ♥

It has been a good winter, not too much snow. Elaine invited me to come to visit her in Mexico and to bring a friend. I thought Anita would need the change and she accepted. We went for March break, since she is still working.

Elaine's place was magnificent, total luxury. We had a relaxing time and it was really good for Anita to do something special now that she is alone.

Amy continues to upset her father when she visits. Unfortunately the upsets have given rise to continuing aggression, on his part. Pushing others and causing concerns for the staff. I saw this at home, with me, however, against other innocent bystanders, it will create problems.

April 2013 ♥

I received a call that they would have to move John to the secure wing. He was exit seeking and aggressive and they can watch him more closely over there. I was really upset and disappointed that he would be losing his nice room. They showed me three rooms in the new section and I chose the one at the end of the hall so he would hopefully have privacy. Many of the residents there wander in and out of others' rooms so I hope to minimize that for John. Two maintenance men helped me move everything over and I spent the day setting up his room once again. It is the same size and there is a living area outside his door which is nice.

He thought it was quite an adventure and he sat and watched me doing everything, giving his usual guidance with every move. There are more mobile people in this wing and I met Carol and Adam. He is farther along than John. She visits frequently and we spend time together chatting and hoping for the best, for both of them. The staff is very patient and John seems to like everyone.

May-2013 ♥

William, our brother, turns 70 this year and Anita, Marie, and I met at his place for his birthday. We had a wonderful time together. We brought lunch and Diane is doing better, however William is pretty well a full time caregiver for her as she has forgotten how to cook and has a great deal of trouble walking.

I have hired Brian to renovate our basement so that the house will be completely finished. That was great fun. I learned how to install a sink and did it myself. I was so proud.

A visit to my heart doctor indicated that there has been no change in the condition of my valves since the last appointment, so that is definitely good news. Next appointment is planned for 2017.

June 2013 ♥

I continue to take John out for drives to the park, Wal-Mart, the Dollar Store and Canadian Tire and Home Hardware. He enjoys walking around and looking at all the tools etc. We usually end up at MacDonald's for a coffee and a muffin then back in time for supper. I have made a few quick trips north as I am renting out the cottage and I need to clean out some old stuff and try to make it appear more spacious. Beth is cleaning it for me, between rentals and Edward and Peter are taking care of the lawn mowing.

July – August 2013 ♥

Marie, Anita and I have planned a four day trip to Halifax to see Robert and Carol. She is wheelchair bound and we plan to take them out for dinner every day and try not to be a burden. Fortunately Robert took the time off so we had a really nice visit. Small trips like this renew my strength and help my blood pressure.

Brian, Beverley, Jack and I took a trip north to assemble a new shed at the cottage. I also had to have a plumber out to install a new water tank and a new toilet. Upgrading is needed to handle the increase in people using the place.

Sept 2013 ♥

We had a cousins' weekend at Anita's and it was wonderful, six cousins together. Later in the month, Brian and I made a trip up to install two new windows in the kitchen at the cottage. We were there for three days. Whenever I go away I make sure that John has company each day I am gone, I don't want him to feel alone. When I return, he just said, "You weren't here yesterday." I reply, "No, I couldn't make it." and he says, "Ok" and we go on to doing other things.

He cannot do puzzles anymore so I am trying different crafts, painting, drawing, writing, tracing etc.

He enjoys a project and is proud of the product when finished. I can see how it relaxes him. The music is the best activity and he sings along. The words are leaving him so most of the time he is just humming and making up words as he goes along.

Oct 2013 ♥

John got into a fight with another resident, Dan. Fortunately Nancy was with John when it happened and she was able to call staff immediately. He came charging into John's room saying,

"The water is rising. Get out, you are being insubordinate…." He had been on a warship in WW II and was responsible for rousting the sailors from their cabins when they took on water. John meanwhile thought he was a Russian attacking him as a child and he came out with fists to defend himself. This happens when two worlds collide. The staff moved Dan to another area, out of the room, next door to John. They avoid each other now. When they meet in the hall, John remembers he definitely doesn't like him at all.

Nov 2013 ♥

Dan has trouble with his feet and is now in a wheelchair so his wandering and shouting are reduced. There is a staff member assigned to him one on one…Dan passed away.

Dec 2013 ♥

John is to be inducted with the 1960 soccer team to the sports wall of fame at the arena in January. We will go to that ceremony. The ceremony is a Sunday afternoon and he will get to see some of his team mates. I think he will enjoy that. He won't go on the bus to any excursions unless I am with him. He is now nervous about leaving the residence. He asked me the other day. "When did we buy this place?" I told him it was a while back and he was pleased saying that it certainly was a nice place and that he liked the people here.

Behind Closed Doors

I plan once again to spend Christmas Eve with him and then go north to spend Christmas day with Marie and Anita. I will return on the bus on Dec 27 to see him that afternoon and New Year's Eve as well.

These special days don't seem to bring forth any memories for him. I have been bringing in albums and he doesn't know what they are about. He will recognize pictures of he and I, but no one else.

Sometimes I wonder if it is wise to try to draw him back, or if it is best to just enjoy each moment because that is all there is for him, at this point.

Christmas was wonderful. Marie had 18 people at her house. It was like the Christmases I remember as a child. We went to visit Grace and Cole on the 26th, they are building a home near Anita and are very happy.

On the bus ride home the brakes caught on fire and the fire trucks came as well as the police. All the riders were standing in the snow just north of the city. They brought another bus to take us downtown and fortunately, I didn't miss my connection. Back in home, Bert and Mary picked me up and I scooted down to spend the evening with John. I think he had a good time. He wasn't able to tell me about it. However there were Christmas cards, there in his room.

January 2014 ♥

I have met and spoke frequently with Candice, Helen and Shannon, all spouses of residents in the secure wing. They all are having problems with children and step children. I guess, they may be impatient for us to die….. It is a shame life turns out this way. At least I am not alone, and that is a comfort.

Lora Kristoff

I am hoping to get the patient care gentleman to help spruce up the area. That wing gets neglected somewhat. I am constantly putting things in order and brought in more Christmas decorations to make it look more festive for the season. Helen and I plan to do more next year....There is an outbreak of the noro virus, a strain of the flu and one is confined to stay in John's room. Not being able to take him out isn't a problem as he doesn't like the cold. The only way I could get him into the car, was to drive it right up to the door.

There are new residents in his wing, Thomas, and James, both are mobile and look perfectly normal. James worked over 30 years in the Glass Plant and lives just around the corner from us. His wife Candice, is having a hard time adjusting, however, knew she couldn't handle things at home anymore.

Sylvia, John's cousin's wife, from Philadelphia, phoned me and we had a nice chat. Her husband, Tim, also had Alzheimer's, as did all four of his sisters. Alcohol took his only brother.

Our friends phoned from Germany and they want me to take a trip to see them, perhaps next year.

Amy and I continue to play musical chairs, however it is less frequent as her visits have tapered off significantly. I really don't want to have them telling me what to do, when to do it and how to do it. I have had a lifetime of that already. I have enough to deal with. They are strong and can face their grief in their own way with each other, which is how it should be. I just need peace.

Feb 2014 ♥

I encountered Amy on my regular visit to see John on Valentine's Day. She was in his room. I walked in, kissed John hello and said to her, "How are you? Would you like to have lunch with your father rather than me?" She replied, "I've got to go." and rapidly left the room. John and I continued our regular routine and had a good day.

He is having toileting issues and is refusing showers so I have started doing them again.

I think he sleeps in his clothes. He is in good spirits and spends a great deal of time in his room. I am so glad that Conrad takes him out regularly, for a change of scene. I haven't taken him off the premises as he doesn't like the snow. There was a lock down due to the flu so I was unable to take him out to the great room and had to stay in his room. We ate supper by the nurse's station on our own.

I had requested that Amy remove her name from our properties, having all the necessary papers prepared at a lawyer's office. She refused, in spite of several reminders. That answers many questions.

March 2014 ♥

For his birthday, I arrived at 10 am, shaved him and got him ready, fortunately Sandra was able to clean him up and change him, so he was refreshed to go out. We met Bert and Mary at a local restaurant and had a nice lunch.

There were singers at the Residence at 2pm and John was happy and sang along with everyone.

At supper time, sadness overcame him and he started sobbing. We returned to his room and he was able to lie down and that seemed to help. Perhaps the day's activities were too much for him. He didn't eat any supper which was fine, since he had a big lunch and I brought in a chocolate birthday cake, his favorite. I left at 6 pm, I was also exhausted.

Lora Kristoff

Thursday March 20 ♥

I arrived and put up Easter decorations in the dining room. When we returned to John's room, it smelled terrible. He had gone #2 in the waste basket, tried to wash his underwear in the sink, pulled up his pants over the mess and he went for lunch. He really fought me to have a shower and change, the staff cleaned and disinfected his room and all was well, when we returned after the shower.

I took his clothes home to wash and his running shoes since they will have to be thrown out. That isn't a problem since I can pick up a new pair for Saturday or Sunday, when I return.

His music seems to be the best way to keep his spirits up and he hums along with all the familiar tunes, since the words are gone.

Patricia has taken to screaming and that angers John and he was ready to hit her, had staff and I not been there. She now has one on one care as she is having a difficult time.

Father Michael went to church on Sunday with John and I. It was the first time Father had been out of the unit, unsupervised. Staff asked me to keep an eye on him and get them if there were problems. All went well. He cried as I walked him back to the unit after church.

April 2014 ♥

I attended the Resident Council meeting. John saw me as I entered the building and was angry that I was so long in the meeting. He was reluctant to go for a drive and when we got the restaurant, he wouldn't get out of the car. We went to McDonald's thinking he would go in to a familiar spot, more readily. He fell asleep in the car and didn't want to eat anything. I drove back to the Residence and the only way he would get out of the car was when I brought a wheelchair for him to ride in. Back in his room, I shaved him and he lay down and fell sound asleep. I left at 2pm. Trudy reported that he continues to resist taking his pills and it is becoming problematic.

I caught a flu virus and was unable to go in for a week. I slipped in for an hour on Saturday before Easter Sunday to bring him some Pepsi and cookies and to check on him. I wore a mask. I am still getting very weak from the virus, however I phoned and found out Amy hadn't been there all week and I wanted him to have some company on the weekend. I will return Easter Sunday providing I am strong enough. The virus has hit me with a vengeance. Wilma told me he had been weepy earlier in the day and she was able to bring him around. He was happy while I was there, knowing I would return to-morrow.

May 2014 ♥

Sr. Joan came down for a visit and I took her to visit John on Friday. We went out for ice cream, drove down to the city park and to Wal-Mart to buy new shoes.

When we returned John was happy with his new shoes and returning to his room,

Eric tried to walk between Sr. and John, near his door, and he became enraged and hit him and knocked him to the floor. John fell half on top of him and we quickly got them separated and John into his room. I think he thought Eric was trying to enter his room and really pushed him away. It all happened so fast. I had slipped into the next room to turn on the music, as that attracts them to go there, rather than into John's room. Everything is so unpredictable.

The head nurse came in and took our statements and this will be another "report" in his file. I washed his feet, changed his socks and put on his new shoes and he calmed down quickly. I turned on his music and he started to sing.

He is just so protective of his space, which I can understand. He has been talking more belligerently lately, so I mentioned to Debbie that it might be wise to watch him as he is quick to move to aggression. For the most part he is happy and I am so thankful that Conrad keeps him company and occupied for so many hours, who knows what would happen if he wasn't there. Amy and Rod told me I was wasting my money hiring him as a companion. That is further evidence that they really don't understand….

I purchases new dolls for John as the others had disappeared. He is happy with them and had them in bed with him squeezing himself onto one small portion that remained. He talks to them and is happy to have them with him. I try to provide whatever he indicates an interest in. Observation is so important.

I went in, on the dentist's request, to take him to have his teeth cleaned. He was very co-operative and all went well. In the past he had always refused care. Glad all was completed without incident. It seems any different experience he needs me to help him walk through it with him.

May 25 2014 ♥

We had a good day, going to church, out for ice cream and to the park for a cool sit in the shade, people watching. We returned and I gave him a reluctant shower. When it was over, he said he felt good.

After a nice supper, John settled down and fell asleep. I was finishing up the ironing and Sam came to the door wanting to come in. I tried to turn him away and had difficulty. Had I not been there, there would have definitely been a problem. I spoke to Karen and the nurse in charge about a possible move to another wing where there are not so many wanderers. I was told to speak to administration, which I will do on Monday.

They moved Sam further away, as an intermediate change.

June 3, 2014 ♥

I received a call last night that he had gripped the arms of Lucy, the night nurse when she tried to take a drink away from him. It belonged to someone else, and had been left on the counter and she feared there were meds in it so couldn't let him drink it.

I spent to-day with John and apart from a real fight to shower, he was generally happy. I was in tears trying to get him to take off clothes he had worn day and night for three days. It was 85, so it was hot, uncomfortable and he was wearing a long sleeve shirt, long pants and a t-shirt and underwear, way too warm for this time of year. He doesn't seem to sense the heat and know how to respond to it. He is losing so many functions. I have to find a way to make showers fun for him.

June 10, 2014 ♥

I arrived and he had had another bm accident, on the chair and rug and floor and all over his legs. The staff had cleaned everything up, however he refused to come for lunch, as he was upset. I went to his room and he seemed to have a cloud over his eyes and there was less recognition. I took the cushion and rug out to the car and brought him to the dining room. He ate his lunch and seemed to recover ok. Apparently he wet himself earlier in the day and the staff recommended that I check into pull ups for him. The home supplies them, however it would be good to have a supply on hand in his room. I am not sure if he will be willing to try them out.

Before supper, Sam came to his door and once again, I had to physically push him out. John was shaking. We sat for a while and he calmed down and Sam wandered off. This was not a good day. There is one good thing. He now will let the staff shower him. That is a load off my shoulders. Now we can enjoy our time together.

Lora Kristoff

June 20 2014 ♥

He has made the move to pull ups for protection. He prefers the briefs so I asked the office to put him on their list of residents needing diapers. He has had several accidents. I have had to wash the chair cushion three times and wash the comforter and mattress cover on his bed. At first, he was embarrassed, now it seems not to bother him.

Sadly, we were looking at the pictures in his room and those in his wallet. I asked who the people were and he said he didn't know. They are all family pictures. Those of myself in his wallet, he couldn't recognize. Mind you, the pictures were of my better days, years back…..I received a call at 9pm the residence telling me that John has been prescribed support stockings, since his lower legs are extremely swollen. I have had to change to sandals because his shoes don't fit anymore. I will choose the type of stocking, when I go in today. I think two or three pair would be advisable as they will need to be washed frequently. His father used them as well, so I guess it is to be expected. He has taken to peeing where ever he is. Not knowing that he should go to the bathroom.

Each day is part of the journey. I did some research and it may be that the Alzheimer's has reached the hypothalamus and thalamus, not a good sign.

His speech is tut, tut, tut with jerky syllables coming out in rapid succession. The expression is still there and he still makes eye contact and feels what he has said makes perfect sense.

July 2014 ♥

He peed in the drawer with all his t-shirts. I had ten to bring home and wash. I picked up a urinal for him to have by the bed when he has to go in the night. Then perhaps he won't pee in all the wrong places.

The doctor prescribed compression stockings for his swollen feet. I purchased some at the drug store and will order the higher compression ones, they are $107 a pair and the union will cover two per year. Each day there is a new experience. His feet have responded well to the low compression socks. They say it is a circulation problem.

We had a near disaster after sitting outdoors enjoying the sunshine. He had an emergency bowel movement and we rushed into the residence and although a little late, avoided a total meltdown. He was shaking all over during the experience and five minutes later it was forgotten. I guess in some ways, forgetting is good. I had considered driving down to the park, glad I didn't. Everything is so unpredictable. I have started to make more frequent visits but for shorter duration, this way I can deal with whatever is happening and get him straightened out and when he is at peace, I return home.

I have committed myself to purchasing a proper sound system for the secure wing, so there will be music everywhere in the halls for everyone. I can't take it with me, so it is good that, giving, will help others.

I write out my frustrations on paper, things I am tempted to say to Amy and Jonathan. I leave the paper sit for a few days and seldom send anything. It just helps me release my stress on paper. With this exercise, I don't carry it around with me.

August 2014 ♥

He won't let staff shower him anymore and got very angry with me when I tried. I got half way through and he threw down the shower head and the fire in his eyes was scary. I just backed off and let him stand for a while. He wouldn't remove his pajama bottoms and went into the shower wearing them, then was angry when they got wet. I dried him off with the soap still on his back and dressed him. I think he feels very vulnerable when he has no clothes on, which I can understand.

The sound system was installed and it is wonderful. The whole wing has playful music in the halls and dining room and it lifts all the spirits, staff and residents alike. They are going to replace the carpeting with laminate this week. That will be great, reducing the odors and making it easier for wheelchairs to move about.

John had been quite lethargic lately. The nurses say he has had a few restless nights, and then wants to sleep all day, to make up for it. A couple of times we have had our dinner in his room since he was unwilling to go to the dining room. His speech is unintelligible, however he still has expression and he makes sounds with such an intensive manner, I know he is trying very hard to express himself. I just try to read his emotions and respond accordingly.

August has been a difficult month as he resists the diapers and also resists being cleaned up after he has had an accident in his bed. The staff is so patient. He got very angry with me and pushed me, when I tried to change him out of his pee soaked clothing. I had found him huddled in bed, complaining he was cold, all the while lying in a soaked bed. Pants, shirt, sheets and under pad were quite saturated. Fortunately the mattress is vinyl. I got his pants off, washed him with a cloth and put on dry pants, then had to struggle to get him to remove his shirt and undershirt which were both very wet. He yelled at me and while I was crying, he finally agreed to dry clothes. It was very difficult to handle. After I leave, I feel exhausted. I am so thankful that there is support of staff.

Amy hasn't been to see her father for weeks. It is what I expected, however, had hoped she would hang in there, for his sake. They were so sure there was nothing wrong, they haven't been any help at all.

At first, I felt angry and disappointed, about not having any support, however in talking with other wives, caring for their husbands, their children also tend to have excuses for not showing up. "I can't stand to see Dad this way." "I want to remember him the way he was." I think they will step up when it comes to their own partners, the generational gap perhaps. One has to let any anger go, as it can eat at your soul.

I know Jonathan is facing challenges as Tony has left home, at the age of 16. Teens think they know everything. Perhaps he will learn some good lessons in the process. I still fear for his safety and the wrongs of society that are prevalent these days.

Sept. 2014 ♥

I have agreed to an increase in John's meds to reduce his anger and aggression. While we were walking down the hallway, Ruth approached us asking about her daughter and John raised his voice to her and I had to hold him back from approaching her with force. He tried to pull away from me to get at her and I was able to hold him back. The road ahead will not be easy. He is starting to accept the use of diapers, thank goodness. He hides the soiled ones around the room so one must search them out, usually not hard to find.

To-day, Sept 12 after his shower and lunch and a haircut, he laid down on the bed to watch golf and clearly, he said, "This is the life." I was so happy to see him so content and at ease. It has all been worthwhile.

I had to bring home his comforter, clothes, pillow and shoes that were badly soiled but I don't mind as long as he is happy. John continues to struggle with accepting the diapers. I finally told him the doctor said he must wear them and he reluctantly co-operated. He wets the bed every night so if he can handle the protection, it will save the staff a great deal of work and clean up each morning.

I was thinking about our relationship over the years and have drawn some conclusions. I loved John as a lover, a husband, then he became very controlling and I endured his controlling demeanor. As the depression set in, I cared for him as a brother. Now, I love him once again as a friend and partner. We have gone full circle. I really enjoy my time with him, as I have found the innocent sweet soul once again and want to have as much time with him, while I can. Life is quite a roller coaster ride. Had I known the Alzheimer's diagnosis in 1995 when the depression started, perhaps I could have separated the behavior from the man and would not have taken his verbal attacks so personally. Hind sight is always 20-20.

Oct. 2014 ♥

I am pleased he is becoming more co-operative in relation to the use of diapers. He really fought with everyone for some time. He is also more co-operative with the staff which is a huge relief. I don't feel quite so responsible for his cleanliness anymore. Emotions overcame me during one of the musical activities and I started to cry. He cried with me. I think in many ways, the understanding is there, at a deeper level. He is so appreciative of everything and now doesn't seem to mind when I leave, as he can entertain himself in his own world.

Nov. 2014 ♥

He continues to be happy as he tends to sing a great deal and he shows pure elation whenever I visit him. It is such a joy to spend time with him now that his anger has gone. The newest development this month is that he now doesn't know when he needs to go to the toilet. He just does his business in the pants. Thank goodness for pull ups.

Dec. 2014 ♥

It has been a difficult journey. He is now wondering what the eating utensils are for. He looks at the plate of food and doesn't seem to know what comes next. Once you start him off by filling a fork full with food, he then can take over. Initiation is the point of wonderment. His face fills with joy when he sees me and it makes every visit pleasant. He still prefers me to shower him and that has to change so I will know he is getting complete care whenever I am not there.

I plan another quick trip north to be with my sisters Christmas Day. I am looking forward to that. I will go by bus once again in the event of bad weather. The trip is relaxing then, warm and worry free. I have wrapped gifts for different departments at the residence. Each need to be recognized for the wonderful work they do.

It is difficult to persuade John to shower unless it is very warm in the shower room. He loves it once he is in there, just getting there is a challenge. Conrad is wonderful with John, so patient and understanding.

Bowel issues are not as explosive as before and that is a relief. He is sleeping more, perhaps after he has had a bad night. The doctor wanted to alter his medications and I refused that option as it was a disaster before and put him under considerable stress and agitation. It is better to be relaxed than anxious, that is what I would want if it were me. The bowel issues are returning, hope we can get that resolved. He spoke with me and mentioned that Lora wasn't there. I asked him who I was and he just smiled. He cannot name Jonathan and Amy in their pictures and he has a more distant look in his eyes. One behavior that pleased me was that one morning he hugged all the staff like family. I know now what they mean as they sense that feeling of community, which is good.

January 2015 ♥

He continues to confuse his days and his nights, so he tends to sleep a lot during the day. Visits are uneventful since he is so tired. I am trying something new in that I go in for a couple of hours in the morning and then return later in the day. Since there is an outbreak of the flu in the residence and Conrad cannot visit, only relatives are allowed in the wing where their family member resides and there is no movement to common areas.

So far the secure wing is a flu free zone. We are very lucky so far. He makes less and less acknowledgement of my company. He is gradually fading in to the distance. He is happy and sings often. The music has been a God send for him. It keeps him happy.

February 2015 ♥

I have been visiting more often as there is a flu lock down and Conrad cannot spend time with John. I have a feeling that, although he is healthy, that the time is short. I don't know why.

This time is precious. He didn't know my name. However he is happy to see me. There really has been a wild ride of emotions. I have drafted so many emails to send to Jonathan and Amy, however I never send them.

I always try to keep on a happy face, for his sake. It isn't easy. I just don't want him to feel fear, that he is alone on this journey. The negative response, to Amy's occasional visits, or "residue", as it has been labelled, lasts for a much shorter period now. She struggles with acceptance and doesn't comfort her father. He only sees someone upset and that is all that she leaves with him. It is unfortunate.

March 2015 ♥

Conrad will be away for ten days so I will cover for him. John cannot control urination or bowel movements anymore. He knows something is about to happen, however has lost the understanding of what should be done about it. The situations, in which he finds himself, upset him terribly. Anticipating a need for toileting, results in an argument, as he will not sit on the toilet when requested and only with much persuasion after the fact, when cleanup is required. I try to smile and laugh to reassure him all is well so that he will accept the support of staff, whenever this happens, when I am not there. I am told he will accept help when he is uncomfortable and is not as resistant at that point, otherwise it can be a battle. I tried to change a dry urine stained tee shirt that he was wearing and he pushed me and told me to "get the f… out", so I did and I went home. Later in the evening when I returned, I washed his feet, changed his diaper and slowly removed the tee shirt. I find he wants to be covered with towels, perhaps for warmth, when I remove clothing. Each approach is different. I am learning every day. It is a joy to see his happiness when I arrive and we spend many quiet relaxed hours together. As I said earlier, this time is precious. He will only accept sponge baths now, so showering is off the table completely, as he will not remove his clothing and gets very, very angry in that situation. It isn't working for now, so it will be set aside.

April 2015 ♥

I have been able to give him a shower about once a week, so it is improving. We are trying medical marijuana to improve his co-operation, so far so good and he sings all the time. It is more pleasant to spend time with him and he still recognizes me.

I have been able to schedule companions for John while I was with Anita, both in Toronto and up north. She was diagnosed with pancreatic cancer April 4, surgery April 14 and home April 24. I have been spending as much time with her as possible to help both she and

Marie through it all. April is a blur. Anita and I cancelled our trip to Europe for May, maybe next year.

I have had to have oral surgery on two root canals. Removal of the pin, bone graphs, a partial plate or flipper as they call it and pegs inserted. There was always a wait between procedures, just another thing to manage.

"If the Lord brings you to it, He will get you through it." (T. Pina)…well He can stop anytime…

May 2015 ♥

Marie had a heart attack May 13 and down to the city for bypass surgery the week of May 17.

I am planning to spend time with her while she goes through this. She has been so tired lately. We should have seen it coming. Our trip to the east coast, in June, has been cancelled, maybe next year. John continues to be happy and I have started volunteering Sunday mornings in the Café to help the ladies out since I am there anyway. Another whirl wind month, one just has to keep putting one foot ahead of the other and be positive in spite of it all.

June 2015 ♥

Both Anita and Marie are doing well after surgery, both at home and slowly recovering. Anita is doing her chemo and so far, all is well. In Florida, Gordon seems to be having health problems with two hospital stays. He may need a complete shoulder replacement. I hope he will take care of himself. All is going well at the apartments, he is so dependable. It is fortunate that he has a lady friend for support.

John had two bad days at the beginning of June, being very difficult with his care. They called me once at 9:30 at night and once at 10:30. They must report his state to me and did finally get his care done, when I called at 11pm. They said they didn't want me to come there since he may associate being difficult as a means for me to appear. I really doubt at this stage he can do that planning. I was just pleased they were able to handle the situation. I know when I do his care, even when he says no, I push through it and get the job done and that they cannot do, according to the rules.

I just heard that Rita is returning to the secure unit, I am pleased since John likes her. Amy didn't visit all the month of May. I know Rodney had his hip surgery so she would have been quite busy.

The doctor increased the dose of the medical marijuana for John and it seems to help. One good side effect has been an improvement in the condition of his legs and feet. The swelling is somewhat reduced.

I am making a concentrated effort to rest more, so I can be strong for myself and others.

John hurt one of the ladies on staff and they have made a referral to the Special Treatment Center. It is a more supportive center focusing on behavioral management. I went there for a tour and it seems nice. There are some similarities to the Grove. Hopefully the transition will go smoothly. I agreed only with the condition that John return to the Grove, following the rehab there. The stay is usually three months and the staff ratio is much better to concentrate on changing behaviors.

In the meantime, I have decided to go and do his care as often as I can, along with staff, so he will get used to a group of individuals giving care. Perhaps we can prevent the move, with this approach.

I requested that the Director meet with Amy and Rod to explain the situation since they will likely blame me for this as well. I am long past the point of being concerned about their opinions since they are rarely there and have not participated in any care giving. The meeting was only to keep them informed since I have consented already. I completely understand the situation with giving care. It is a real challenge, every time.

There is a return to the seraquil medication as the sepraxa doesn't seem to have helped his compliance with care. I had noticed that he was more hyper with that med so the return to the former med is likely for the best.

It is wonderful how they watch and monitor each resident so closely. The Grove is a wonderful facility.

The move to treatment may take a while, since there is a waiting list.

July 2015 ♥

There have been changes, he is more confused and seems restless. His legs are still swollen. He still is happy to see me and appreciates all the attention. His co-operation with staff is limited. He has gained weight so I have purchased more track pants as well as tear away pants. I hope that they will make changes easier.

I have had to increase my duties with care as he is particularly violent with the staff. They approach him and he becomes very defiant, he even tried to punch Wilma, his favorite PSW. He has forgotten how to go to bed and must be shown how to lie down and take his shoes off. He sleeps in his clothes, as changing him is out of the question. I was called in to sign all the papers for the transfer. I thought all the paperwork had been done, it is now July 13. It will likely take a while.

I received good news. He is not the top priority for moving. Another resident is more in need of the special placement. It seems his move may be postponed. I want him to stay, so I plan to do more to give support to the staff. I have been going in and doing care three times a day. I want him to get used to the idea of the cover up, (half a housecoat) which makes him feel covered and a little less resistant. The move would be so upsetting for both him and I, new environment, new staff, routines, not to mention the problems cleaning out his room, clothes, furniture, television etc.

August 2015 ♥

Things are pretty much the same. He still sings and recognizes me when I arrive. I appreciate this each time I visit. I know it won't last. I visited a medium and his father had a message for John. He said he was waiting to welcome him along with his mother. He was to choose the shining door. There was a concern with his heart, even though he doesn't have any history of such difficulties. Spirits from my family sent messages of strength and support, particularly my grandmother. The medium assured me, love lives on and his spirit will always be with me. That helps me as I face this challenging time with him. She assured me to attend to the children as one would, dogs barking, just let them be.

I have been going in every morning about 7am to do his care. Each day is very different now. I have found him on the floor, half naked with feces on the floor, another time, asleep peacefully, and sitting asleep in his chair. Apparently he spends many hours through the night wandering. I realized that he has forgotten how to go to bed and must be guided through the process. It is taking longer to calm him down. Music still helps.

Aug 20 ♥

This morning I had a dream that he was lying beside me and it was so real I reached out to touch his shoulder. It is a comfort, as I feel he will visit me, in spirit, after he passes.

I have suggested that they do the care and I just be present. Hopefully we can make the transition to total care done by them. I go in and help with care in the morning, and again at 7:30 pm, so he starts and ends his day in comfort. It turns out that I need to assist with the care, in order for there to be co-operation. He is a big man six feet tall and at about 200 pounds, when angry, is a force to be reckoned with. I hope it will be possible to make a transition soon. Even with my help, Aug 24, he punched the nursing assistant and had a very wild look in his eyes. Perhaps he feels cornered, with so many people pulling at his clothes. I just don't know what will work. Going in frequently seems to be starting to work (Aug 27).He is much more at ease. It is very important to me to prevent the move to treatment, where everything will be strange for him and I would think, frightening. Last night he turned to me and as clear as anything said, "thank you". It brought me to tears.

September 2015 ♥

Wilma and I were able to do his complete care in about 5 minutes and he was happy throughout the entire process. He is also co-operative with Lily. While she and I were giving him a shower, I said, "This is Lily, she is one of your girlfriends". He looked at me and replied, "Yes, but I don't know what to do." Such a precious moment… I think we are starting to turn the bend…Sept 11, There has been a change in his condition. He has stopped singing and humming. He walks quite stooped and eye contact happens occasionally. He was looking out the window and he said, "Anya" and other sounds that were unintelligible. Anya is Mom in Hungarian. I asked if he was talking to her and he said "sometimes". He is happier and more co-operative with me seeing him every day. I think his fear is subsiding and he is more at home now than before. At the dinner table he needs to be prompted to eat. It is hard to watch the steady decline.

Amy hasn't been to see him for a month now. I realize she has a hard time dealing with her grief.

I have sent off money birthday gifts for all the boys, it will bring them some joy and let them know I am thinking about them. I am meeting Marie and Anita at William's for a belated birthday gathering on the 24th. William and Diane are quite excited about our visit apparently. I am determined that John should be comfortable and feel safe so his journey will be experienced without fear. The swelling of his lower legs has disappeared. I still have him wearing sandals all the time as they are easy to wash and that needs to be done frequently.

October 2015 ♥

There has been a significant change this month. He needs to be fed, just sitting there unable to decide what to do with the food placed before him. He is distant, frequently gazing into space. He has mentioned his mother a number of times and said he saw her. I will have spent an entire day with him and at some point in the day will turn to me and surprised say, "Oh you are here." His music is disappearing as he is unable to carry a melody as he did previously. Now he hums sounds without a tune, self-stimulating vocalizations. I have been giving him his care for many mornings and I am there to put him to bed at night, this way I know he will have a good sleep to prepare for the next day. He, often times will not acknowledge others that he knows in the café. He seems to be drifting away more and more. He has started "chipmunking" or pocketing his food in his cheeks, not swallowing it. Apparently this is another stage. He also now wanders into other rooms, not aware where he is. The half housecoats also seem to make the care process more acceptable to him. He frequently cries when he sees me, so I am constantly reminded that I must be there for him. I know he would do it for me.

He is completely lost when trying to find his room. He talks to the pictures in a magazine and smiles, he prefers pretty women.

He will hold a sandwich, placed in his hand, and will eat it on his own. Perhaps this motor memory from carrying a lunch pail to work, for so many years, is still there. He doesn't seem to know the function of a fork, knife or spoon. He still smiles and says "that is good" after tasting Pepsi, his cold beer, chocolate or a caramel candy. These small pleasures bring him joy.

In Florida, Gordon had his shoulder replaced, six weeks in rehab, and will have extensive therapy to gain mobility once again. He wasn't able to drive when he got out. With health care drivers and friends he was able to carry on and oversee whatever needed to be done down in Florida. Repairs now are minimal, fortunately, with all the work that has been done. I am considering finding another maintenance person. However it doesn't seem fair, with him having so many health issues. Postponing a change seems the best option for now.

November 2015 ♥

John now calls me Mama. Perhaps he has forgotten my name. It is good that he sees me as someone that helps him and takes care of him. The staff is now stepping up with care which is a relief for me.

He started swearing at me when I removed his pants at bed time. Emotion is still there, then it is quickly forgotten again and he is happy. Anger stays only briefly. Music continues to soothe him and he moves to the rhythm, dancing. I start noticing what remains, rather than what is gone and that is good for both of us.

My friends continue to give me encouragement and support. Time for laughter is much appreciated. I find I cannot rest until I know he is in bed at night. Knowing he is asleep is a comfort. I noticed he looks into space and tends not to focus on the television anymore. He continues to drift away. He now mouths objects so I have to watch what he has in his hands. One day I emptied my change purse since he tended to like sorting and piling coins, when I noticed he had put coins in his mouth, I realized that that activity wasn't appropriate any more. I purchased a muffin and coffee for both of us. When he had finished the muffin, he picked up my reading glasses and put them in his mouth. Another example of growth in reverse, I think.

They have asked me to put on the wrap around diaper at bed time as it is easier for them to change and it is more absorbent than the pullups. I understand and will start doing that from now on. He had a facecloth in his hand and put it to his mouth, trying to bite it. I have been watching him more closely the last few days as he hasn't slept well and is difficult to engage in any interaction. I wonder where his mind is. Conrad continues to provide support and he engages him in as many activities as possible. If unwilling, he just sits with him and that is fine also. I have stopped going in in the mornings as Jane pointed out I have to trust them to get the job done or I will have a heart attack since I am taking on too much, going three times a day. Now I just go in from 3 to 6pm, for the supper feeding and to settle him for the night. He has been taken off the list for a move to treatment. I am told it is due to the changes and the time I have been able to devote, calming him down.

I am spending time with other residents and getting to know their families and that is a big help since we are all going through the same struggles. It is a support system that just happens. The staff is really overworked. However they are doing the best they can. There are 13 residents on the unit that need feeding help. I usually help out where ever I am needed. Some say I should be on staff. John has accepted the wrap around diapers even though they are bulky and tend to ride down. That shows me he is farther along than expected. Distraction is the key to care, putting a candy in his mouth, a sip of Pepsi, holding his hand or singing to him, all help with getting care done. Amy hasn't been to see him since Aug 12.

Jonathan and Anna are separated. He and Tony are living somewhere, in a condo some distance away, no word from any one. I guess an alteration in my POA and executors would definitely be in order. They will not be here for me, that I know for sure. It may be that they will regret not being there for their father after he is gone. It is hard to say, everyone is different. I am really fortunate to be close to my sisters and also to have so many friends. Laughter has helped me through my very low times. We go to movies and day trips. Book club helps and visits to wineries. There is a great deal happening in the area, a very wide selection which fills a day and diverts my attention for a while.

Good news, the staff was able to do care and put him to bed. When I arrived they sent me home to "relax" for once and take it easy. Sometimes even that is difficult.

November 18 ♥

Last night he was sleeping with his eyes open. I don't know if this means some of the automatic responses are being affected already. I gently closed his eyes and he didn't reopen them while I was there. After I shaved him, the next day, he tried to drink the shaving lotion. I quickly handed him the Pepsi bottle and he was happy again.

I find the wrap around briefs difficult to put on as one has to hug his hips to get a proper fit. He is easily distracted now, so care isn't such an issue. Nov 24: Yesterday he started to eat the Noxema that I had out, to put on his feet. I had washed his feet and cut his toenails and the Noxema was on the bed beside him. Before I knew it, he had put his finger in the jar and put some in his mouth.

Amy and Rod visited to-day, returning from working down south apparently. There was some "residual effect" which quickly disappeared after their visit. I suppose they are home for the US Thanksgiving. Good that they were able to spend some time with John. Their visits are in the middle of the day, which is his optimal time of day. Her understanding is still limited, regarding his experience, what they see, is such a tiny slice of the picture. It is too bad she has missed some of the joy he has been able to share with me. Those moments are special and help with the grieving process for me, knowing he is in a comfortable place, free of stress, anxiety and depression that he had for so many years.

December 2015 ♥

Each day I can see him getting weaker and weaker. His legs and arms are very thin as he has lost muscle mass. I am pleased that he settles quickly to sleep each night, often sleeping with his eyes open. He laughs and smiles at many things around him. I am not sure what sparks that joy. I just go along with it and share the happiness with him, whenever it appears. I am glad that sad moments are very brief and are few and far between. I must be thankful for small blessings. He is completely co-operative with me now, doing care with others present. I am still putting him to bed each night.

June, a neighbor friend, passed away. I am going to the wake and the funeral Dec 8 and 9. She was only 78 and a wonderful person. I know Andrew will have a difficult time without her.

Dec. 8 ♥

After shaving John, Connie came to help me change him and as she entered, he wavered and fell to the bathroom floor. I was able to break his fall, however couldn't prevent it. He hit his head on the wall on the way down and lay dazed on the floor while we got help. Connie cleaned him up and changed him, while on the floor and they brought in a lift that hoisted him up to his chair. He turned a terrible yellow color and was like a rag doll, throughout the whole process.

I know balance can be an issue in late stages so I will look into the possibility of the temporary use of a wheelchair. He is quite unsteady while walking and with his height and size, falls will be hard to stop, trying to prevent injury. I alerted Conrad so he will be watchful from now on. The OT approved a transfer chair to be kept in his room, on loan from Victoria, to be used when he is unsteady.

He now considers the staff his family and smiles whenever they speak to him, also calling out to them as they pass. Conrad continues his wonderful support and we have worked out the Christmas schedule.

Dec 16 2015 ♥

Amy and Rod were to visit John and I had her help with a diaper change. We were civil and caught up on some of the family news. They said they will visit him on Christmas day while I am north so that will be nice. I am glad Helen is on duty Christmas night, Thomas, is on Christmas day and he and John have been doing exceptionally well, John likes Helen, and I am sure she will get him to bed without any problems. I just like to know that he is comfortable each night. Conrad and his wife, Joan, have the flu so he will not see John until the New Year. That will double up my duties. I am trying to stay healthy and rested so I will not fall victim to the flu this season.

Amy said they would be there Dec 23, a no show. Fortunately, Tony, a volunteer, took him out and he had a good morning, without them showing up. I will have to learn to not expect anything, so I will never be disappointed. Sometimes I struggle with understanding how they deal with the grieving process, however I have to put it out of my mind and focus only on John's needs. They are adults, with independent lives and judgements. I don't have time to deal with them, at this time. Their support would have been welcome but that wasn't in the cards.

I had a wonderful trip north. It was great to see everyone and the weather was perfect and dry highways. I picked up Don and Valerie midway, so I had company for part of the trip and we returned Dec 26. Amy and Rod did come Christmas Day and the staff said he seemed to enjoy his meal with them. It is good they gave him that time and I could rest easier knowing he wasn't alone. He couldn't remember any of it when I asked Dec 26 in the evening. I realize he now lives moment to moment which is stress free, I would think.

Frequently when I am spending the day with him, all of a sudden he will still turn to me and say, "Oh, you are here." It happened three times the same day and each time he was very happy to see me. He emulates the joy of a child at Christmas and that is good. I am getting to know all the residents and they seem to think I am coming to visit them as well. Ruth said when I arrived, "Thank goodness you are here." Jessie said, "I have been looking all over for you and here you are." I try to sit and talk a little, give them a magazine or toy and then they are on their way again. So many residents are alone.

To-day, Tanya and her service dog, Oreo, stopped and spoke with John and me. She said that she had observed that he is totally engaged when I am with him, in comparison to times when he is with others, in the café. She said, "He is more alert and alive, when you are here." It brought tears to my eyes and John, sitting beside me, couldn't understand my tears and started rubbing my shoulder to comfort me. It is so ironic that he is aware of my need for comfort, while he is the one set adrift. One never knows what life will bring. She loaned me a book describing a wife's experience with her husband's Alzheimer's. I found it helpful.

I still go in every night to put him to bed. It seems to relax him and it is also a comfort for me to see him at rest. He has started stiffening up when I try to assist him in laying down. After doing his care, we sit on the side of the bed, then I remove his shoes and holding his shoulders say, "room train" German for turn around, "hin leegan" lay down and "tv showen" watch tv. I have written the phrases on paper on the wall above his bed for the staff. Spelling the phrases phonetically aids in pronunciation. Slowly he seems to get the idea, patting the pillow behind him, he will notice the intent and when he decides, he will co-operate. Sometimes it takes a little while. Once lying down he tends to ignore me and watch the golf channel. It is on day and night. Last night I sat on the side of the bed and he said as clearly as can be, "You're beautiful." Moments like that are very special. The amazing part is that most of his language now, is humming and unintelligible. On a few occasions he has said, "I love you." When that occurs, all the hard times living through his depression, anger and paranoia seem to disappear and one appreciates the soul that is still inside, trying to deal with the wonder of it all.

I have been enjoying time with my book club, one afternoon a month, breakfasts with the golfing ladies, fish and chips on Friday nights and regular visits with Bert and Mary. They are always busy with the grandsons and family events. It is nice to relax and share updates from time to time, usually once a week. Bert has been giving me some of his red wine which I enjoy before going to bed. Friendship is so important to help keep your sanity. They have been with me through this entire experience. It started with Bert spending evenings with John while Mary and I went to movies, just so I could get out of the house for a couple of hours. I spent quite a few evening crying, even back then. They are the only ones that saw what was happening and understood the many sides of John. Bert told me later that he had said to him on one occasion, "I don't know what is happening to me, but I can't do what I used to be able to do and I don't want Lora to worry." He also said, "I have cobwebs in my head." That was when he remembered that he couldn't remember. He is becoming very unsteady on his feet, shuffling down the hall. I am glad he is in good spirits.

….I returned to his medical records and found the first prescription for Lorzapam, it was 1995, twenty years ago. Understanding that depression and Alzheimer's go hand in hand, explains a great deal now. The doctor's notes were, "extremely anxious." 1996 prescription for luvox, "anxiety/depression".

Trying to understand and live with depression was challenging for us and it certainly tested our marriage in many ways. I had seriously

Behind Closed Doors

considered leaving him on a number of occasions, since it seemed that I wasn't able to bring happiness into his life. I never could bring myself to do it, always holding on to the hope that it was a "chemical imbalance" or some other health related issue that was changing him so drastically. I always, perhaps from my mother's example, put on a happy face, trying to be an "Unsinkable Molly Brown", (life boat 6: Titanic). I shared none of my struggle with anyone except my sister, Anita. I couldn't say negative things to Amy or Jonathan about their father, therefore no one really knew about the difficulties dealing with a partner's depression. Over twenty years of challenge and more to go.

January 2016 ♥

I continue to go in each day in the afternoon and then back again at night to put him to bed. We have established routines now that he is comfortable with. Gradually, I am hoping staff will take over this bedtime duty as well. For now I am doing it, I guess, for myself, to be sure he is settled and relaxed. He still shows such joy to see me, it warms my heart. It seems, the man I married is gradually returning, before he leaves for good.

The Alzheimer's society told me you will grieve twice, all the time during the journey and again when he passes. My recreational reading has been somewhat philosophical to enable me to see the broader picture.

I came down with the flu. It was a dandy bout. I was weak, dizzy and slept day and night. I called in each afternoon to check on the bedtime routine the night before and of course Conrad watches over him during the day. Thomas, the RNA, handled things wonderfully well. He has developed a rapport with John. I will be sorry to see him go. He has a permanent day posting at The Pines and leaves the end of January.

Conrad is so thoughtful and offered to bring by some groceries, if I needed anything. Fortunately I was already stocked up and really didn't feel like anything more than soup and hot drinks.

Anita's cancer is back in more of her organs. She is in hospital. The cancer has reappeared in her left kidney, her spleen and her liver and lymph nodes. We will know what the plan is next week from her oncologist. She will have to decide the course of action she is comfortable with.

I missed three and a half days with John, he was happy to see me when I walked in and we got back into our usual routines again. I am still very weak. The nurse practitioner at the doctor's office said the flu is going around and will likely last for a week. There is an outbreak in the secure wing, so residents are confined, with family still able to visit, fortunately. I visit Mary and Bert regularly and speak to my sisters often, particularly now with our concerns for Anita. She stayed with Marie for a few days and will, whenever she doesn't feel strong enough to be on her own. Her friend, Allan, has really stepped up and is helping her a great deal. Everyone is so happy for the two of them. They dated in teenage years and now both 70, have found one another again.

John has been fortunate with avoiding the "bug" that is going around. I have my fingers crossed. The last few days he hasn't made any sign of sudden recognition when I arrive. Perhaps I am now just another face in a maze of faces that greet him each day. He is however grateful after I have done his care and he is clean and dry once again. I have some concerns about the frequency of their checking on his care. I know they are consumed with those that are ill on the wing.

I have accepted the position of secretary with the auxiliary at The Grove. I am there so often, I don't mind helping out. I work in the café, help with birthday parties and provide support with feeding at supper time. I may be involved in booking entertainment for the monthly birthday party.

We are going to try showering John while he is seated in the showering chair. It has been recommended since he is sometimes unsteady on his feet and that would prevent the chance of falling while in the shower. It is also regulation for staff to always use a chair, so this will be the final move to staff taking over. They want to try showering him in the mornings. I asked them to postpone that move until I had established a routine with him and have had a number of PSW's with me to gain familiarity. Wilma and I did the first one together, without incident. He did well using the chair and seemed to enjoy the experience. I will assist for three or four more showers, so the transition can be accomplished.

I received a call that they had tried to shower him Jan 28, on their own. They hadn't checked my requests to be in attendance, and failed in their endeavor. I took care of it in the afternoon. Sometimes requests don't get recorded or read, I am not sure where the miscommunication ocurred. Jenny helped me with the shower. He resisted and I persisted, and it was accomplished. They need to be aware that change is very difficult for him and he requires a great deal of gentle persuasion to go a new direction. He was very happy and comfortable for the rest of our afternoon and evening together. He is becoming quieter now as verbalization is greatly reduced. When he tries to communicate something, his face is very animated. Replies such as, "Is that right", "I didn't know that" and "I will take care of that right away" usually satisfy him, and we carry on.

Anita called to give me an update and I have promised to meet her in the city, when they discuss the trial research possibility. She is going to have a cancer driver bring her down from the north and I will meet her there. It will be sometime in February.

February 2016 ♥

John has allowed staff to shower him twice, while sitting in the chair while I was present.

I will attend a few more times and hopefully the transition will be accomplished. During the day, he turned to Conrad and said, as clearly as can be, "You are the best". Both he and I were thrilled.

I am finally at the conclusion of the oral surgery procedures. Now Dr. Adams will attach the implants and I can be done with the flipper. Dr. Harriman was wonderful. I was put out for the first procedure and for all the others freezing was sufficient. Ellie and Bev helped, with driving me the first time, then after that, I always went on my own. I didn't want to have to expect someone to wait for me each time. There were six surgeries in total.

Wonderful news, the staff was able to shower John without me present. I was thrilled to hear the news.

Anita went to see the oncologist. She doesn't qualify for the research trial and has two or three months to live.

I made plans to spend time with her giving her support.

I am going to have staff put John to bed every other night so he gets used to them, then when I am with Anita, he will be accustomed to my absence for a few days at a time.

I decided to drive up north Wednesday afternoons and return Friday afternoons. This way Anita can spend as much time as possible in her home and if the boys wish to join me, I can pick them on the way and take them back down on Fridays. Anita has been spending her weekends with Allan. Marie has extended the invitation for her to stay at her place, whenever she wishes to. We will just follow her lead, to assist her any way we can.

I called William, Robert and Grace to give them the news.

I have started to let staff do the evening duties, spending afternoons only with John. I find I am very tired and I want to be strong for Anita as well. Everyone reminds me to take care of myself and that, I am trying to do.

Grace called and has suggested a cousin's weekend with Anita, Feb 27-28. I will have to work around a few things, but I will manage it.

I have been using the transfer chair to take John from the wing to the coffee shop and back again. It makes doing things easier and he seems to enjoy the ride. Amy hasn't been to see her father since Christmas. I emailed her to request visits, while I am north with Anita and no reply. I have decided to completely accept the fact that she or Jonathan will not be there anymore. When all is said and done I guess a couple is always really on their own, regardless of past memories. We lived and loved for each other and so it will remain. Any other attachments were small benefits, to the entire package. Giving to others was what we enjoyed and that is enough. I have a favorite poem called,

<u>My Cup Is Overflowed....</u>

...If God gives one strength and courage
When the way grows steep and rough
I'll not ask for other blessings
I'm already blessed enough
And may I never be too busy
To help others bear their loads
Then I'll keep drinking from my saucer
'Cause my cup is overflowed.
(John Paul Moore)

March 2016 ♥

John told me tonight as clear as ever, "I love you". Everything is as it should be. This time is so precious.

Anita has just a few days left. I have been visiting her, cleaning out her house and gifting articles to special people in her life. She has been completely clear mentally and that is a blessing. They continue to up her medications, to prevent any pain. I came home for the weekend and John was doing well. He also was getting weaker however he was happy to see me and was fighting a cold so he was quite tired. I have been diligent in getting rest to keep my strength up, taking one day at a time. Don, Anita's youngest, has been a wonderful help through it all. I returned north, prepared for her last days. She went to hospice. It is a wonderful place and everyone helped all of us deal with the process. The boys are taking it hard and all saw her, March 8.

She passed away March 9 and the funeral was March 12. It was a difficult day for many people. There was a large group of visitors and that was a true tribute to her, as a wonderful person.

It made me thankful that John was still with me in spirit and body, with his mind, caught somewhere in between.

I returned home and fortunately he had been doing well in my absence. I phoned frequently to check up on him and was always reassured that all was well. I will have to go north fairly often until the house is emptied and on the market. The executor duties seem overwhelming. I am sure all will work out in the end.

We celebrated his 80th with cake and friends at the residence. He seemed to enjoy it. Bert came and he recognized him. It was hard for him to handle, seeing John like this, I could tell. He has been such a wonderful friend for many, many years.

I return north for the Easter weekend to tackle the house, cleaning, painting etc. Grace and I are hoping to get a substantial amount of work done. The night before I left to go north, John said to me, "We were lucky" and I replied, "Yes we were." Then he was gone again and I put him to bed and settled him for the night.

We were able to empty the house, clean it and list it with real estate.

April 2016 ♥

We have multiple offers on the house and it should be sold today, April 11.

I have been visiting John daily since Conrad is in New York with his family for a week. Somedays John is there and others, he prefers to sleep. He is still happy to see me and that makes it all worthwhile. He is co-operative with all the staff now and that is such a relief, giving hugs frequently, to special ones. It has taken almost five years but I think we have arrived at last…I am finally able to relax and feel at ease with his situation. I think now I go in more for my benefit than his. It is so hard to let go.

It is enjoyable to see him relish cherry pie, so much so that he picked it up like a sandwich and was concerned when I tried to get him to return it to the plate, perhaps thinking I would take it away from him. There is still some rational thought going on, with regards to food at least.

He still enjoys the music and laughs frequently. Anxiety is seldom seen. Tears come when he sees me. We share many hugs and he holds tightly onto my hand. He is peaceful when he falls asleep, then I go home.

I am going north for two days to meet with the probate lawyer and the lady at the bank regarding Anita's estate account and other papers to get the process moving along. The boys have been very helpful and that is good.

May 2016 ♥

The eldest sons are particularly anxious for the estate money. Don and I are going up May 23 to finalize things and hopefully it will be done with soon. I have received many calls reinforcing the fact that they want to see <u>all the accounting.</u> They don't trust me. Usually when one cheats others, you expect others to do the same. I understand now, a small portion of the stress Anita had to deal with.

John is doing well. He laughs a lot and is still happy to see me. He has spoken a few clear sentences amidst a jumble of words. When I was changing him, he said, "What are you doing?" I was amazed at the clarity. The next moment it was lost again. Amy came Christmas day and one day in March and no sign of her since then. I am not expecting anything anymore so if she or Jonathan should appear, it will be a surprise.

I sent a money gift to Tony for his high school graduation…also no response. The silence speaks volumes.

One of our longtime tenants, Victor, in Florida also has Alzheimer's and I have contacted his family in Illinois to come and get him and take him back with them. I hope that will be done this summer.

Someone told me that the soul chooses how it will move into the non-physical and with Alzheimer's the choice is, for a long good-bye. It is also a peaceful transition. Hearing that, was a great comfort to me and I am glad we are having our long good-bye, as we all will travel the same path sooner or later.

June 2016 ♥

John is doing very well. I still go and put him to bed every night. I hope to gradually move away from this custom so the staff is able to take over. I have had two staff members on different occasions watch my routine so I hope the transition can be made without too much difficulty. I think I go in for my benefit more than his, since he has spoken clearly to me a number of times. We have danced to the German music and we have cried together. I wouldn't miss this for anything.

A thank you card arrived from Tony with a short note.
I am driving north for one day to inter Anita's ashes and have a small gathering at Marie's afterward, June 24.

July 2016 ♥

John has an attraction to pretty women in magazines. He talks and laughs and kisses them with pure joy on his face. I held up a picture, asked him to stand and he promptly did. He particularly likes Jennifer Aniston. Now he and I, and his "girl friends" move around the residence together. I am so pleased he finds happiness in simple things. The innocence is beautiful to witness. He continues to be co-operative with staff and all is well.

The Forgetting Forgotten Father

You used to run to me shouting, "Daddy", with pure joy upon your face
The love and happiness we shared, I thought nothing could replace.
Are they so busy? I am never on their mind.
Had I broke my back, rather than my memory
Would you still walk away, leaving me behind?
One loves and cares for children, giving them all I did without,
It's a surprise and disappointment. They walk away, leaving me in doubt.
Come and sit with me briefly. Talk to me and hold my hand
I'd like to say goodbye to you. I'll try to understand.
I know it hurts to see what's lost. I'd be there for you, no matter what the cost.

That's why I don't understand. Do you blame me?
This path was in God's Hand.
Although I cannot say your names, You've forgotten, I'm still me.
I still see, feel, laugh and love. Within my heart you'll always be,
I'll watch over you from above
You know that I'll forgive you. My love's too big for hate.
I'll see you again, When we meet at Heaven's gate.
I know I'll leave soon, There'll be no need to cry.
I've had a wonderful life with you.
I just chose a long good bye.

You might say this poem was somewhat inspired if you believe in that possibility.

It came to me early in the morning and just "fell" into place. It is hard to explain.

Perhaps I feel the children will really regret missing this wonderful experience with their father. I feel it is a great privilege. Having lost Anita, I realize how precious life really is. One takes so much for granted.

July 12 ♥

I had changed John and was dressing him for bed when he looked over my shoulder and seeing the pencil drawing of Jonathan and Tony, he smiled and said with love, "Jonathan". I said yes and then the moment was gone. There have been other clear moments. I was tidying up his room about 6pm and he said to me, "Are you going home?" I replied, "Not just yet, I am going to sit with you for a little while." I sit on the side of his bed and hold his hand until he falls asleep. He holds my hand so tightly even after he has drifted off. I have to pry my hand from his. It seems he is trying so hard to hang on to our reality. It is hard to let go. All these moments are so special to me.

I met with administration July 13, to try to solicit more help for the PSW's in the secure wing. It seems there is little to be done other than advocate to the government, the administration had answers for everything and none addressed long waits in wet diapers so I will continue to provide the care, I feel John deserves and I would hope, I will receive, when I am in a similar situation. No additional staff for the secure unit and more needy clients waiting in the wings.... 10 to one, 15 to one and 30 to one at times has become the norm. In his unit, 15 in wheelchairs, 12 feeders, 20 with behavior issues etc. only three out of 30, that can communicate their needs. Child Day Care have 5 to one ratio and must be toilet trained. These precious souls cannot talk, have large bodies and are on the downward trend of the learning curve. They need care.

I bit the bullet and formulated an email to the authorities regarding the ratio of PSW's to residents. Victoria and I have put in on Facebook. Hopefully it will get some attention.

It has been a heavy week since Conrad was away.

July 17 ♥

John had a fall, bruising his elbow and perhaps hurting his back a little. We were fortunate that he didn't hit his head. He continues to be unsteady on his feet, gradually getting weaker.

I sent the Forgetting Father poem to Amy and Jonathan. I hope they come to see him while they can. I received a call from the Alzheimer's society. They are going to publish my poem, "Forgetting Forgotten Father"

I told Conrad the news and he was very supportive encouraging me to publish more. I am seriously thinking about it.

I went north for two days for Mary and Andy's wedding (Marie's granddaughter). Everything went well and was a really nice break. I have invited Marie to spend the winter months with me and perhaps receive the dialysis here. It is quite a challenge for her to stoke the fire all winter and I know we will have fun together. I think her children were happy to hear the news. I know it will mean distance from them however it will take a load off of their plates for five months of the year. She is going to-day to get a port put in her arm in readiness for treatment. It is supposed to heal before commencement, we have our fingers crossed.

John was happy to see me when I returned. He hung on tightly that night, as he fell asleep. I talk constantly while I am with him, hoping my voice will reach through the fog, providing him with some comfort. Perhaps it is like rubbing a clear spot on a frosty window, allowing sunlight to shine through briefly, to the other side.

We have had some hardships in our relationship. However we endured, now 46 years later, we arrive at the period of transition. I am so lucky to have my sister and brothers and so many friends that have provided support through it all. I have been working on putting all my affairs in order as Anita had. This will make it easier for Grace, when my time comes. There are so many details in one's life, more than I realized.

August 2016 ♥

Aug. 7 when I sat with him and he hung on tightly to my hand and arm, he said to me, "Love me forever." It took my breath away. I assured him that there was no question about it. I believe his spirit will always watch over me and that is so reassuring. That is Faith.

I am checking on wheelchairs since he is unsteady on his feet. I am pleased he has no pain.

I sent an email to Amy with an update and a reminder for Jonathan to cash the check I sent for Tony's university.

I was able to find a wheelchair for John and purchased a new cushion and two covers for the seat so there will be a change when necessary. He really likes it and smiles whenever we are "cruising" down the halls. It is the appropriate size for his height which is very helpful when transferring him. Marie spent at week visiting with me, going to the residence and we sampled many restaurants while she was here. We had a really great week.

September 2016 ♥

I am trying to stay away and let the staff put him to bed so he is accustomed to someone else once in a while. I am having the routine colonoscopy so I will be away from him for the prep day and the day of. Life just goes on.

I haven't been to Florida in over a year with Gordon and Julia doing such a good job taking care of things. He slipped and fell, cracking his left pelvic bone and was in rehab for a couple of weeks. Fortunately, he didn't fall on the shoulder he had replaced recently. It is my hope that I may be able to take some brief vacations with my girlfriends, going south, and perhaps renting the unit, to help with expenses. Fortunately Gordon's lady friend invited him to move in with her, so that has solved the accommodation issue. It seems the maintenance is getting to be too much for him, a change may be in order.

John had a fall and bruised his elbow, other than that, he seems in good shape. He is stiffening up and moves very slowly. I try to get him out for a walk, on nice days. He pushes the wheelchair as we walk around the parking lot. The wheelchair just steadies him. Grace, my cousin, spent two days with me and we had a wonderful time. Every family seems to have its drama. It is good to hear that of others. Then you don't become overwhelmed, with your own. What a relief….when you are not alone. Timothy passed away at the residence. Victoria and I have become good friends providing each other with company and support. I know we will keep in touch. I am so fortunate to have made so many new friends over the past five years.

Amy called and I spoke with her and Rod, on their speaker, for about two hours. They apologized for things that happened and I felt numb, knowing they had not been there with any support. I feel it is best they continue with their lives and I with mine. However, they do want me to help Tony with university costs. We will see how that turns out. It was evident that they had been drinking as they repeated ideas often, slurred their words and even got upset about who should say what, telling each other to be quiet, while the other spoke. It was interesting. They are doing well with the business and that seems to be their focus.

October 2016 ♥

I arranged a lunch with Amy and she didn't show up. I had asked her to name the day and said I would be there. She expected an email confirmation, therefore didn't appear. I tried again with a lunch another day, to be able to speak to her when she was sober and it turned out ok. She spent all the time talking about the business, Jonathan, Anna and Tony so I just let her get it all out. It was apparent that she would be very reluctant to spend time with her father, so I kept quiet about things that were happening and realized that I would continue to be alone on this journey with him. It is good that their business is doing well and it keeps her busy.

Jonathan continues with his challenges in marriage and raising Tony. I feel it is best not to comment or get involved. Trying to assist in the past never turned out well, so I plan to just let it be and let it go.

John is doing well, is happy and co-operative. I am pleased that he is not creating any problems for staff anymore. I had an 8 day trip to Germany and thoroughly enjoyed the break and meeting with our friends. John's companions visited mornings and afternoons while I was away, texting me with updates, it was great.

Upon my return, I went north to close the cottage and spent some time with Marie for a day and a half. Victoria rode with me part way, to visit her brother and sister in law, Timothy's brother. The trip went fast with our chatting all the way. She has a way of lifting spirits and is a positive person to spend time with.

It is becoming fall now, with cooler days and trees are beautiful and life goes on.

Everyone keeps saying to get a life of my own and to get out and do things. It is not easy, thinking that I should be with John, while I can, since time may be short. Afternoons with my book club, evening concerts, lunch with the golf ladies, all are certainly very refreshing and I am able to push the guilt aside for a few hours.

November 2016 ♥

Victoria and Rose and I planted the daffodil bulbs in the courtyard. They will look nice in the spring. John was with us in the courtyard, supervising all the activity. I think he enjoys watching new and different things. The weather was perfect, in the 60's, unbelievable for November. I had a sign that there is still comprehension. With the extreme warm day and the activity, I was in short sleeves. John had a shirt and sweater on, sitting in the wheelchair. As I approached him, to move him closer to the activity, he took my arms and rubbed them with a concerned look on his face. He was obviously worried that I was cold and should have a long sleeve sweater on. Although he couldn't say the words, he understood. That evening after changing him, brushing his teeth and having our customary waltz in the room, he said, "love you". Moments such as that make everything worthwhile. I am assured he is happy wherever he may be on his journey. This is a long goodbye and now I feel it is a blessing.

The evenings are the best as he is relaxed and has more focus it seems before going to sleep. We had completed our routine and he was in bed listening to the German music and he opened his arms, drew me close and just held me to his chest for about two minutes. I felt he was truly with me for a while.

I emailed Amy, for another luncheon for my 70th birthday. I thought she would likely be home for the American Thanksgiving, no response in 2 weeks. Being an optimist sometimes really sucks…☺

I am sure he hears and understands. After cleaning him after a particular messy situation, he said "thank you".

Later, when relaxed in bed, he said "many problems". His facial expressions are clear and warmth felt when he hugs me is very real. I read in a book in the Great Room that memory is not needed for love. That is absolutely true.

My birthday, Nov 22, lunch with Amy didn't happen. I requested she remove her name from our Canadian properties, to allow financial decisions needed, regarding our care, could be made by me, when and if necessary. She indicated she was upset she had been removed as my POA. I explained to her POA's need to be able to visit, care and support those in their charge, acting in their interests, not in her own personal interests. She is unable to "handle" seeing her father, therefore caring for the financial and personal needs, being an advocate for me, wouldn't be possible. She became quite upset. I had misplaced our trust and now must deal with the aftermath. We will survive. In many ways the lessons learned, are quite a revelation of the human experience, many twists and turns no one could have anticipated. This is life.

December 2016 ♥

I have spoken to Marie, letting her know I will not be going north this Christmas. I don't know why but I feel I need to be here with John. In the past, I had spent Christmas Eve with him and Christmas day with Marie and Anita. This year is very different. He is more distant now and it took about an hour for a sign of recognition. Although still happy to see me, I notice a significant reduction in focus.

Conrad has been struggling with health issues, so I suggested that he only spend mornings with John or if need be discontinue. He has been such a wonderful support, for both John and I.

His health issues have subsided and he will continue full time with John. When he was leaving, I sat next to John and he smiled and held out his hand, grasping Conrad's arm, laughed and shook his arm saying goodbye. It was beautiful to see.

John is very content in the wheelchair and when standing it takes him a while to gain his equilibrium. I try to walk him everyday up and down the halls. I do enjoy the phrases that pop out unexpectedly. Every day is a new day. Our bedtime ritual is very special for both of us. The best part is a slow waltz to the German music. He has a broad smile while participating. Music has played a very important role in his relaxation and comfort. I noticed he is mouthing objects, something a very young child does to experiment with the environment.

Learning is in reverse. I continue to be pleased that he is comfortable and happy. On our walk from the dining room back to his room, I noticed he was considerably stooped and shuffled as he walked. We took several rests along the way. He had another fall, scraping his scalp. It was not pretty, however healed quickly. I emailed the Christmas pictures of John to Jonathan so he could see how his father was doing, even though a picture really doesn't give too much information. No response.

Lora Kristoff

January 2017 ♥

We have established a routine that seems to keep him happy. I enjoy giving attention to the other residents as well, so many don't have company. John had another fall. Losing his equilibrium seems to be more common now. This time he scraped his right arm and elbow. I must be always vigilant while he is out of the wheelchair, as any turn, could result in a fall it seems. He is so co-operative now with care it is hard to imagine the challenges we had, getting to this stage. In many ways it is wonderful that one quickly forgets the negative and in place of that, savors the positive that follows. He still holds my hand tightly as he falls asleep each night and that is the reason I feel I need to be with him, perhaps not so much for him, as for myself. I read that the one remaining may need to give the other permission to let go, as the two souls are trying desperately to cling to each other. That is much easier said than done. Facing our mortality is certainly a "wake up call", no pun intended.

Physio asked me if I wanted John to be restrained in his wheelchair since he has had 5 falls in the last three weeks. I made it very clear that I didn't want that and that he is perfectly happy sitting all day in a chair provided his "care" has been done and that he stands and walks around only when he is uncomfortable. The diaper rash must bother him and the frequency of changes is a definite issue. I was suspicious of them "forgetting to change him" and so I marked his brief at 11:30 when I left, returning at 4:30, there had been no change. I hit the roof as nine hours from 7am to 4:30 is totally unacceptable. He is now on a toileting and walking program. Another home has been in the newspaper for violations and so the response was quick. Hope it lasts. I said I need to be able to trust that his care is done and then my worries are reduced since it is their responsibility. I never mind doing it myself when I am there, that is not a problem, however if I need to be away for any period of time then there may be need for concern.

He was confined to his bed and room for two days with vomiting and the runs, so they wanted to prevent any spread, in case it was contagious. He was content sleeping and watching golf. He needed the rest and I fed him toast and juices, hoping he could keep it down. The third day he was up and moving around and eating the regular diet. He is much thinner now and I continue to be vigilant while he is walking. The whole home is on lock down with an upper respiratory problem, so activities are limited. He continues to be happy and content.

February 2017 ♥

I had a concern about his fingers turning a blue color. Apparently his oxygen levels were between 75 and 80 and should be at 90 at least. His hands are frequently cold and there seems to be no explanation for the discoloration. Staff put him on oxygen overnight and by morning levels were up again. The condition seems to come and go. The first Friday of every month they have "Italian Hour" in the Day Program. A gentleman comes in and plays the accordion. Conrad took John over to listen and he was laughing all the time and got out of his wheelchair to dance to a polka. I was working in the café and missed the experience. I was so happy to know he had such joy.

One of the PSW's shared an experience she had with him in the middle of the night. She was working the night shift and went in to check on him. Finding him awake she sat down and talked with him. She said he talked and sang songs until he drifted off to sleep again. It is so wonderful to have such caring people available to give him company and support.

Feb 16th ♥

John has a chest cold, seems weak and sleepy. The most alarming thing is that, when helped up out of his wheelchair he was unable to keep his equilibrium to stand without assistance. It is my hope that the cold will dissipate and he will return to his happy self. I was unable to get him ready for bed on my own.

March 2017 ♥

On March 1st we were sitting out in the Great Room and John had fallen asleep as is his custom in the afternoons. I was sitting next to him holding his hand and reading my book. He opened his eyes, smiled and said, "Beautiful". He let go of my hand and put his arm around me and drew me close to him. It took my breath away. Moments like that are so very special. That evening after feeding him supper and walking him down to his room, changing him, washing him, cleaning his teeth, shaving him and tucking him in to bed, he reached out once again and drew me close to his chest. I could feel the sincerity and warmth of his embrace and he was with me for those few moments, then he drifted away once more. All the hours with him are so worth the knowledge that from time to time, he knows me and senses me near.

There are also times of laughter, while hugging me before going to bed. He did what he always used to do at home, during the hug, I noticed, he was looking over my shoulder at the golf game on television….typical male.

Our cousin Grace is undergoing brain surgery, microvascular decompression, to relieve headaches and facial pain she has been experiencing. We all have her in our prayers.

All went well and she is on the road to recovery. She was very fortunate and is happy it is over.

I attended a workshop on Forgiveness at the Learning Center. I knew I had to work things out and release anger and disappointment on taking this journey, without family support. I learned a great deal and feel better about the position John and I are in. It was meant to be this way and letting go of the past is the way to go for me. I cannot change or control the choices of others and knowing I couldn't have done this any other way, is a great comfort. I have done my best. If I were faced with this situation once again, I would follow the same path, there is comfort in knowing that and sensing that there are no mistakes in this world. Choices are made on all sides of any situation and the only ones you have to live with are your own.

April 2017 ♥

The physio therapy staff is starting a walking program for John since he is a little too comfortable in the wheelchair. He enjoys the extra attention and is doing well. He continues to say stray phrases in German that are appropriate to the situations. These "break throughs" as I call them, are always a pleasant surprise. His tried and true character traits are still evident. He straightens my shirt, jewelry that is twisted and wrinkles in the covers… there should be order in all things. I feel these are all signs he is very much with us still. I have noticed he is moving more slowly now, and it takes a long time to walk to his room. He likes to stop and rest along the way. He is less engaged with what is happening around him. Conrad continues to be wonderful, providing smiles and support each day. I don't know how I could have managed without him.

April 24 ♥

Amy, Rod and Jonathan called me about 9:30pm on Sunday night. I was asleep and it took a while for me to focus on their message. Basically they attacked me once again, why did you do this, why did you say that, why didn't you explain etc. I reminded them that we hadn't moved, they were welcome to visit their father any time and I had expected them on his 80th and 81st birthdays and they chose not to appear. Unfortunately, Amy had been drinking, repeating herself often and not hearing any message directed to her. I can tell they are hurting. I explained to them that Alzheimer's isn't an easy road to follow, but we must deal with illness as well as health and take what comes our way. I am just doing the best I can, and my focus and attention are on my husband, and my personal health, and they are welcome to support us, if they choose to. They are still on the path of grief and I understand. In the early stages when I tried to talk to Amy about her father, she wasn't ready to pay attention to the message and always brushed it off, so I just let it go.

April 27 ♥

I fell off a ladder, landed on the grass fortunately, and sprained my ankle, no broken bones, just needed an air cast on my ankle. I am now called "Hop along", had the cast for three weeks, much better now, however a bit stiff. Driving the car with my left foot was a little tricky. I am such a rebel, still needing to visit John.

May 2017 ♥

It is starting out as a rainy month. Everything is green and alive, spring is here. I get the air cast off on Wednesday and may have to have physio. It is getting better but still not 100%. I am able to walk John to his room now and get him ready for bed on my own. I have developed a routine that he enjoys and we sing and dance during and after, as we move toward the bed. He continues to hold onto my hand very tightly until he falls asleep. Those moments are special. Conrad has been away visiting his sister since she is not well, so I have had double duty, mornings and afternoons. He is back on Monday May 15, thank goodness.

Mother's Day, no messages…I think now that the whole situation boils down to me not doing what Amy and Jonathan wanted me to do, care for John, on my own, at home. I knew from my research that I could not and should not, try to handle everything alone. Our history had always been that I "fixed" things throughout their childhood. This was something I couldn't fix.

Physio came and requested that I look into a larger wheelchair for John. He has been slipping forward, since the seating area is not large enough and his legs are so long. Occupational therapists have been requested through CCAC, to take proper measurements. If I cannot find a chair on my own, I will order it through the government, since it will likely be one for the long term.

June 2017 ♥

John has lost his equilibrium and can no longer stand on his own. The home provided a larger loaner wheelchair and to prevent him slipping forward, having a four point "seat belt" keeping him in position. John doesn't mind it and this chair has the reclining feature that he liked in the other one. I returned his first loaner chair to a local charity, donating it back to them. That is a wonderful place. I have contacted the union benefits to see if they will pay for the part of the new chair that the government doesn't pay for. I feel that this will likely be the spot for him for the duration so I want to get the best. A Broda chair seems to be the top of the line. I still have to wait for Occupational to meet and measure him. It seems I am learning something new every day.

David, a friend of the family, moved into the secure wing, and sits with John in the dining room. I think John recognizes him as he has attempted to talk to him and smiles when he sees his sons. John coached them both in soccer so many years ago... 70's I think.

I have started the process of trying to sell the property in Florida. We will see how that goes with Amy and Jonathan.

Amy refuses to sign the listing agreement so I will keep the apartments to the end.

John enjoys going outdoors and sleeps peacefully in the shade for an hour or so. There have been special moments when he reaches for my hand and pulls me in close, to hug me. I know he is there and appreciates my support. Those moments make it all worthwhile.

Marie had vascular surgery in the city and I went up and spent time with she and her daughter. All went well fortunately, hopefully she will be starting the dialysis and return with more energy. The low kidney function results in her sleeping a great deal, there is one good thing in that, she has no pain.

It continues to amaze me how John holds so tightly to my hand as he falls asleep. It seems he is clinging to our reality and that is wonderful. I am pleased that he feels secure and safe with me by his side. When one cannot communicate, you learn to read every gesture with very close attention.

I had a wonderful day with CAA on a day trip to the theater to see Guys and Dolls. It was a show that made you laugh and was truly uplifting. It was a wonderful day. On my way home, after the bus dropped us off, I drove down to check on John, at 8 pm, he was sound asleep.

July 2017 ♥

Summer has arrived. It is hot and we are having beautiful days. Many days I take him out to the courtyard for fresh air and he tends to fall asleep, quite comfortably. He shows little interest in the tomatoes and peppers we planted. Andy Peters has moved in, father to three sons, all on John's former soccer team. It is nice for us to see familiar faces. It is becoming like old home week. It is a comfort that we are not alone on this journey and we can encourage each other along the way.

July 6 ♥

John said my name, I was talking to friends and he called for me to return to his side. It was a complete surprise and so wonderful to hear... Conrad continues to give such positive support. His companionship, I am sure, has definitely been an important variable in keeping him alert and focused. July 7, I was trying to feed Ned when John said, "Bliebst bei mir" "Stay by me", I couldn't believe my ears. July 8, he said, "I love you". There are so many signs that he understands and those moments are such a gift. July 14, when settled in bed he turned to me, squeezed my hand and said, "Thank you". It was amazing.

August 2017 ♥

August 3, it was a very hot day, I was reading to him in the courtyard, he fell asleep in the shade and upon awakening he grasped my hand and said, "I like you." The same day after helping with his care and putting powder on his private parts he said to us, "That's better now." When all of his communication is a collection of sounds, expressions and pointing at things in the distance, those clear phrases are truly astounding.

Occupational Therapy measured him for a new chair. It will take two weeks to arrive. I have tried to order the options that will anticipate his needs both now and in the future. He was laughing and happy with the attention and shocked all of us by pulling open my blouse and taking a peek, then giggling at the opportunity. Quite a guy...

Lora Kristoff

September 2017 ♥

It has started off as a beautiful month, weather wise. I will try to enjoy it as long as it lasts. I flew down to Florida and drove our van north. It had been on loan to Gordon, as part of the maintenance agreement. His van had been t-boned while he was picking up a dryer for us, sometime ago. It is a shame he seems so lost and had difficulty giving me directions on driving him back to his girlfriend's home. I had noticed his memory slipping for some time now. I gave him a severance check to help him out for awhile. Hope all goes well for him. I hired a new maintenance person, Sam. He seems very nice and was recommended by Andrew. The new kitchen, in one of the units, is almost finished, just waiting for the new counter top to be installed. Michael, the new tenant seems very patient. He doesn't have to leave his old place until Sept 30, so that helps.

John did well in my three day absence and continues to be happy. Conrad has been away visiting his sister, whom has had health difficulties. Fortunately, everything seems to have stabilized for her and he will soon return. I know John will be glad to see him. He still recognizes familiar faces and enjoys the company. We continue to take one day at a time. He was thrilled to see Conrad again. He just shook with excitement, it was quite an experience.

Donna has returned to work in the secure wing and John really seems to have an attachment to her and she can settle him with the evening routine. Hurricane Irma swept through Florida. Fortunately there was no damage at the apartments apart from the power being out. We were lucky.

John continues to surprise me with short comments spoken at appropriate moments. "That's good" after a drink of beer, "You are leaving now" after he was in bed, "Das ist furuck" that is crazy "Wo sind sie" where are they "You are here" "I love you". He tapped my arm when I was feeding Ned, letting me know he was ready for his next mouthful. I have been reading information about essential oils and have initiated daily application of frankincense.

I am walking everyday with friends, started a body stretching class and enjoyed my first monthly book club meeting.

October 2017 ♥

I have had to find alternate companionship for him. Conrad was asked to leave, due to his involvement, helping other residents. One thinks helping others would be appreciated, however there are so many rules and boundaries that I am not aware of. I will miss him terribly. However I feel he needed to take a break as he has had considerable stress with his family and daily visits at the home are definitely emotionally draining. Perhaps it is for the best, as I could see his time with John was taking a toll on him. Fortunately John seems happy as long as someone is close by, anyone. I have organized morning companionship only, as he is tending to sleep most afternoons. I am going to withdraw from my volunteer hours. They were starting to overtake me and saying no is not one of my strengths.

I feel good about my decision, as my focus will be solely with John, as it should be. Spreading oneself too thin, taking on problems of others, happens slowly, but can consume you, before you realize it.

November 2017 ♥

He has become somewhat weepy since the medical marijuana has been cut off due to supply issues. He is also showing some stiffness in his joints when changing positions. One never knows, what change is "side effect" and what is "progression of the disease". I will be spending two days in the city when Marie has her eye surgery. I hope all will be well with John. He is so content when I am with him it is hard to stay away. He holds on so tightly to my hand while I am there.

Marie's surgery was successful, apart from many follow up appointments she is doing very well considering all she has gone through.

After considerable thought I emailed the following to our children:

Update and thank you:
Unfortunately, anger rose from deep grief for everyone, I understood what was ahead and you didn't. I didn't believe in 2006, understood in 2011 and you didn't believe in 2011 and understood in 2016, that's ok.
This family runs away and they don't talk, that's ok, it's who you are.
After discussing estate planning and taxes with our accountant, he suggested that selling would simplify things as we went over returns from 1992, relating to the apts. I also thought Jonathan would appreciate receiving part of his inheritance now when he needed it. You are welcome to discuss it with the accountant, to hear the reasoning behind the idea. US/Canada estate resolutions are extremely complex. Waiting isn't a problem for me.
It seems you make assumptions and jump to conclusions, only reflecting who you are. It doesn't matter to me what you think or say about me since it is only your reality, not mine.
I view life as a glass half full and make the best of it. I accept that both of you left both of us when we needed you. I am thankful to know now, rather than later, when I might have been helpless. It's ok. Plan A didn't work, on to Plan B.
We are doing fine. Your father is doing well. He enjoys his new chair, smiles and holds my hand tightly till he falls asleep. Occasionally he says phases that fit the situation, pleasant surprises from time to time. I can tell when he is there. These are bonus days for us.
Rodney can take care of both of you now, I appreciate that. We worried about both of you for too long.

Time to let go.
The boys are young men now and capable of making their own way.
Wishing everyone all the best, just giving you an update.

This marks a turning point for me as I let go of all that was, and continue to do whatever I can, for the two of us. The grieving process is a long journey and not an easy one, however life goes on.

Dec. 2017 ♥

John has adjusted well to the new companions. They report he enjoys his hot chocolate and people watching out in the café. I find that he tends to sleep quite a lot in the afternoons while I am with him. He is verbalizing less and less, however he holds my hand tightly while I read to him and even when asleep. I wanted to change positions while he slept and he just held on, as I tried to move. That tells me he knows I am there. Giving comfort is all I can do, at this point. He settles quickly at night.

The television is left on the golf channel day and all night, without sound, so that if he wakes up he can watch the beautiful scenery and he has light in his room. He had been afraid of the dark before so I think it is good for him to have that reassurance. All is well. I have decided to remain here for the Christmas season. Marie is busy with her big family and the one day north creates issues with bus schedules and weather related worries that I don't wish to deal with at this point. I am working at reducing stress as much as possible. She and I talk regularly on the phone and it is becoming a pleasant "visit" for both of us. All went well with Christmas, had a wonderful meal with John and joined our friends' gathering for some Christmas cheer in the afternoon.

I continue to walk 5 km each morning with Ellie and Sandra. It is a struggle to get there for 7 am. However I am glad after and feel so much better for the rest of the day. I am making a concerted effort to maintain and improve my personal health, for the long run. There are a number of good movies that the girls are going to which will provide levity to our days. I am planning to take two lady friends to Florida for a quick trip in January. They are so excited. Having fun things to look forward to continues to be a priority.

January 2018 ♥

The doctor has reduced some of John's meds so he isn't sleeping as much. Reduction must be done gradually so his body will adjust to the change. Everything seems ok as they asked me to watch for any reactions that may occur. He is quite alert and actively watches television laughing at different situations.

Andrew, one of the RNA's reported his clear sentence. While applying some cream to a minor infection in his private parts, he clearly said, "What the f###k?". We laughed, as his response was very clear and very appropriate to the situation. The only concern at this point is a rattle in his lungs, which seems to persist. I requested cough meds. An x-ray has been ordered, we will see what shows up.

Marie had a scare and was in hospital with a cardiac "event". With alteration of some meds she stabilized after a week of unsettling incidents. All is well it seems and she was sent home.

I went to Florida for four days with the ladies. We had a wonderful time and I was able to take care of a few issues at the apts. Sam is doing a great job with maintenance and I am very pleased that worries there have diminished significantly.

John is slow to recognize me now and once in a while he will reach over and touch my head gently or hold his arms open for a hug. Each time is very special for me. Sensing that perhaps my voice reaches through the fog, allowing a small familiar memory to penetrate the darkness where he lives, gives me comfort knowing that the hours are well spent. My goal is that he moves without fear, knowing he is not alone, for those moments when he is present in the here and now.

February 2018 ♥

I believe that love is a feeling transmitted through presence and that is enough. In my ongoing quest to find solutions, one never gives up hope for the one you love. I listened to a doctor's account relating to her husband with Alzheimer's. She advocated the keto diet heavy with coconut oil since she reasoned that the brain needs fat of that type to communicate within itself. She stated that the brain is made up of fatty tissue and coconut oil given to her husband, seven teaspoons daily had resulted in steady improvement in his ability to draw a clock and in his speaking ability. With nothing to lose, I have been giving John coconut oil mixed in pudding daily for the last two weeks.

Last night as I was wheeling him down to his room to prepare for bed, I stopped and gave him a big hug and kiss and he smiled and said, "You're crazy". I was floored, since he hasn't spoken clearly to me in a long time. It was wonderful. It was so encouraging since I know he is hearing me and is aware of my presence. He continues to hold tightly to my hand throughout our visits.

I am pleased that I have given up the volunteering at the residence since I was too busy there and neglecting my time with him. Life goes on.

Feb. 19 ♥

Family Day. I had a talk with John telling him it was ok if he wanted to leave, even though I wanted him to stay. He seemed to understand. I told him the children would be ok and I would be with him in the next life as he had been with me in former lives, as well as this one. He would continue to be my angel on my shoulder so we would always be together, where ever he is. I told him it would be ok and not to worry about me as I would be talking to him, as he is always just a whisper away. He seemed relieved and immediately fell asleep. My continuing anticipation of a possible break in the cloud, as light shines through, hopefully provides a sense of love and support. He is slipping deeper into the veil.

March 2018 ♥

His joints are stiffening up and one must gently pull his legs to straighten them when he lies down in bed. He still searches my face for reassurance as he is lifted up, when transferring. He has such a look of wonderment and happiness at each little adventure. It amazes me that, his grip on my hand remains so tight even when his breathing tells me his sleep is deepening. He continues to enjoy the personal attention with his companions, money well spent. I am just so thankful there are people available, to pass time with him, when I am not there. My time with friends gives me strength to enjoy life and face new experiences, without a partner at my side. That is an adjustment after our near 50 years together.

We are booked for many shows at the theater, Operas at the Cineplex, ongoing lunches and dinners and short trips to Florida, Kentucky and Quebec. I don't like to be away more than 4 or 5 days at a time. Our friends have invited me to Germany in the fall. I will have to think about that. Ellie and I have planned the Germany trip for August. We are very excited about it. I took Dr. Bernard's advice seriously, he said, "It is imperative that you take good care of yourself." He was so helpful.

Another lady was recommended to me, to be a companion for John. This brings the number to four. I think it is good to have many options since each have ongoing commitments, they need to attend to.

March 24, a big day, I was hugging him and laughing and tickling him and he said, "I love you." It took my breath away. Amy made a surprise visit on his birthday. It was in the morning and he slept through it. It is good she made the effort.

April 2018 ♥

We have settled into a routine that is working very well. The companions for John are wonderful and he is very happy with all of them. We enjoy quiet afternoons together. I read to him, he sleeps at times holding my hand tightly even when dozing. From time to time he will reach out and stroke my hair or the side of my face. He is very calm during those hours and I feel this is when he truly knows that I am there for him. He continues to show great joy when I arrive and it is all worthwhile.

May 2018 ♥

We are fortunate to have four lovely women to visit with John mornings and afternoons, when I am unable to make it. I try to be there as often as I can to sit with him in the afternoons, feed him his supper and tuck him into bed. I have also recognized the need for me to spend time with friends. Shows, the opera and plays, all are welcome respite. I am confident that John is in very good hands while I am taking care of the cottage and the apartments' maintenance issues. Brief trips north, provide me with some time with Marie. She is facing health issues as her kidneys are failing. It is wonderful that she has family support and is in very good spirits. Girlfriends accompany me south on short trips and we enjoy laughter and silliness together. Friendship and sister support are wonderful.

In thinking about the whole Alzheimer thing…. It has been good, in that it has provided John with an escape from the stress, anxiety and depression which he suffered with, for so long. He is at peace now and finds joy and laughter in all the little things that make up life.

June 2018 ♥

I had a 4 day trip to Florida with Ellie and Sandra and had a wonderful time. Upon my return I spent a quiet afternoon with John and while watching golf in his room, usually, he sits quietly in his chair with hands folded in his lap. This time he raised his arm, put it around my shoulders and drew me to his chest. There we sat for about a half hour before he moved again. I am so thankful for those moments…

He is now on ground food as he is starting to have difficulty chewing and holds food in his mouth longer than needed. I recognize that this is another step the next being puree then liquid. I am just so pleased he has no pain and he still knows when I am there.

July 2018 ♥

John is having many good days. His four "girl friends" as I call them, continue to be his companions when I cannot be there. It is such a relief to me to know he is not alone and they are entertaining him and getting him involved with whatever activities are scheduled. He always greets me with a smile and occasionally a hug in return for my hugs and kisses. He giggles and knows I am there, either that or he thinks "who is this crazy woman that keeps coming back?" either way it is fine with me.

Unfortunately Ned passed away, it is hard for Terry. We had become close friends, facing the same trials. The people I have met here have really enriched my life and I am very thankful for all of them.

Since John, being wheelchair bound, is not a flight risk anymore they have offered a move to another wing, which is not a secure wing and the residents are retirees with different care plans and much quieter. I decided to accept the offer, since the room faces the road and he can watch cars going by and there is a really nice living room outside his door, similar to the one he had in his first placement. I will miss the sweet innocence of those further along the dementia path, in the secure wing. I think he will be happy in his new spot and fortunately we already know many of the staff in that wing. David, his friend, is also there.

Ellie and I have scheduled a trip to Germany, after an invitation from our friends, to celebrate his 82nd birthday. We are going for 8 days. I don't want to be away any longer than that. My supports are in place, mornings and afternoons while I am gone so I am sure all will go well.

August 2018 ♥

Ellie and I had a wonderful time in Germany. Our friends made us feel so very welcome, all went very well. The family entertained us and we visited many old friends.

John was very happy to see me upon my return. He has settled into his new room. That wing is quieter. We return occasionally, to visit our friends in the secure wing. I also accompanied him to his bath. It was a wonderful experience. He really enjoyed it, seemed so relaxed, smiling the entire time.

I have been reading about Alzheimer's and that choice he made, for the preparation for his transition, into the non-physical. He lived through a long period of depression prior to diagnosis, creating so much stress within his mind. Alzheimers gave him relief from worry and stress from his past and helped him find peace. At the same time he wasn't ready to leave just yet. That reading has helped me appreciate his presence and his happiness with all of the wonderful innocence and love he can still express. I am thankful he isn't ready to move on just yet and that I have so many wonderful hours with him through all of this. Just one example: He reached out, took my hand, brought it to his lips and kissed me. He is definitely still there. …

William's wife, Diane passed away at 84. She had been bed ridden for some time and long term heart difficulties plagued her after her aneurysm. He has been a tower of strength by her side. Robert is flying in for the funeral so it will be nice to visit with him. Marie, Grace, Robert and I will be staying at the same hotel near William's place so Marie will have a place to rest and still attend. I have lined up John's visitors while I am away overnight. I have added two new people Sandra and Evelyn. Both think he is great and enjoy seeing him smile. He seems so content. It is heartwarming. It was good spending time with my family. We were able to catch up on news and share memories that are near and dear.

September 2018 ♥

We have settled back into our routine and John seems to like his new location since this wing is quieter and no one wanders into his room. We have adjusted his schedule, so that he has a nap in the afternoon after lunch, rising about 3 pm. This is good as it provides him a change of position, out of the wheelchair, an opportunity to stretch his legs and enjoy a sleep. Quite often I arrive early and read to him and wake him gently just as would have happened at home. Amy and Rod visited Sept 13 for a while in the morning. I was told he seemed to recognize them. I am pleased that they spent some time with him. Sandra, John's companion, left them alone, since it was her visiting time with John. All worked out well.

I emailed Jonathan to let him know that his father has started to refuse solid food and that they have him on a liquid supplement. I felt they should know in the event there is a further turn of events, just wanting to keep them informed. Rod, Amy and Jonathan conference called and wanted more information so I told them my understanding of the situation. They thanked me for the update and Jonathan said he would plan a trip north. He called on his own on the land line also, while I was at Bert and Mary's for our Thursday supper night and I returned his call, with more explanation. He is coming north Oct 3 to Oct 6.

I have let him know John's schedule with his visiting companions, so hopefully we can arrange quality time for him. I am glad I made contact and that they are responding.

October 2018 ♥

Jonathan, Rod and Amy visited Thursday, Friday and Saturday mornings. They also visited for Thursday and Friday afternoons. John seemed happy they were there. It was good that they saw the feeding issues that have developed. I was able to explain some of the journey we are on and they listened and were grateful that I had let them know. I am pleased that I have had time and been able to have distance, from their grief. It has made me much stronger and confident in my own self-sufficiency, as I know that is what I will face in the future.

Friends have provided me company, diversion, laughter, support and future plans for when I am on my own completely. I have also received very good advice about saying yes to all invitations and weeks fill up with many things to look forward to. I took an overnight trip north, spent a day with Marie and a day at the cottage watching window installation and putting things away for the season. There was snow in the air, quite a surprise. I return, Oct 22 with three lady friends, to close it for the season and a small holiday. It is such a beautiful spot, we have enjoyed for so many years. There are so many things that bring back good memories. It is comforting to realize that good memories last and difficult ones fade quickly.

November 2018 ♥

John has experienced a severe rash. I ordered the shingles shot fearing it may be shingles similar to what his father had experienced in his later years. The doctor says it isn't shingles. It is spreading despite two prescriptions of creams and a change of body wash. He is on a rather strong antibiotic due to the infection in his private area and this hasn't had any positive effect on the rash. I am going to try washing his shirts at home, along with his johnny gowns hopefully that will help. I may also try coconut oil lotion. I have requested antihistamine each night to reduce the discomfort of itching that he is experiencing. It seems that one must watch so many things when communication is not there.

Speaking of communication, he has been saying more phrases: What is happening, hello buddy, what the f... are you doing (while having a bath), why etc. There is always a surprise for staff and myself. He made the thumbs up sign also. If he has had a series of strokes, along with Alzheimer's, there would be no change in the care plan. However that could explain his ability to verbalize spontaneously. Strokes usually have a window of recovery.

He looked at me with the tenderness that is difficult to describe, leaned toward me, opened his arms, pulled me close and kissed me full on the lips…I was dumb founded and overjoyed…I just know he is still in there.

Amy and Rod visited Nov 18, at breakfast time. It is good that they spend some time with him. I feel no anger anymore, no disappointment anymore, and no expectation anymore. It is a good place for me to be.

December 2018 ♥

I developed quite a chest cold and stayed home to recover. I didn't want to take the germ into the home. His four companions took over with visits so I was comforted that John wasn't alone. It is flu season and everyone must be careful.

Our friends, in the residence, have invited us to join them with their Christmas celebrations. They are being so kind and understanding. David, their father has adjusted quite well. He is 90 years young and has many moments of clarity.

Thursday December 6….John said my name. I had been sick for four days and Thursday afternoon finally I was on the mend and visited. That was a very special day… I know at many levels he understands. He held my hand tightly and put his arms around me when I hugged him. Once again it took my breath away. These memories will live forever…He continues to battle the rash around his neck and arms, creams and changes in soap and antihistamines have not been too effective, still a mystery.

Thursday December 20....I was feeding him his supper and quietly he turned to me and said, "Hast du schon gegessen?" "Have you already eaten?"

December 24.... Rose was giving him his bath and as he was being transferred in the sling from his chair to the tub, he said, "What are you doing?"

Words and phrases are appearing more frequently so every day is an adventure.

January 2019 ♥

He is more verbal now than he has been in a while. He moves his feet as if he is ready to march away. He laughs frequently and his rash is gradually going away. I have started washing all his shirts and johnny gowns at home and that seems to have made a difference.

Jan. 7 upon waking from his afternoon nap, he opened his arms and I hugged him and laid my head upon his chest and he started laughing out loud, a laugh that was accompanied by him holding me tightly. I am so pleased when I can experience his love once again.

His infection in his private area has returned and is starting to cause him considerable discomfort when he urinates. The doctor told me the only way to prevent this recurring is circumcision surgery. He told me that he will have pain for a couple of days following the procedure, however in the long run, will cure the situation. Although it is a difficult decision, I know it is for the best. Consultation at the hospital and patient transfer are arranged for January 30 and hopefully surgery soon after, prior to recurrence of infection. He has just finished a ten day dose of strong antibiotics and they are reluctant to make antibiotics a regular plan as that has negative effects on his stomach and in the end, will reduce immunity. A merry go round it seems.

Surgery is scheduled for March 20, with another pre-op trip, prior to that, for blood work and EKG and a meeting with the anesthesiologist, that date will be arranged by the hospital so a total of three trips to the General. He is in good spirits however seems to be sleeping more now. I suppose it is peaceful for him. Sleep is such a nice escape.

February 2019 ♥

We have developed a routine that is comfortable with John having an afternoon nap each day with me feeding him lunch and dinner. I stay and relax and read by his bed and it is a quiet time for both of us. It is really very good.

March 2019 ♥

All is on schedule for the surgery. I had a surprise. I was laughing and joking with John as I tried to feed him, he is reluctant to open his mouth wide enough for a spoonful of food. I winked at him and he winked back. I know he was playing with me.

I had a pleasant surprise, Wednesday, March 20 when I arrived at 8 am to get John ready for the big day, Amy and Rod were in his room, thinking they would visit and feed him his breakfast. I explained the plan and they stayed until we headed off to the hospital at 10:30. Surgery went well, if that is possible, in any case. He is in a lot of pain. Surgery was delayed two and a half hours which necessitated a change in patient transfer time. The transfer bus doesn't pick up after 6 pm so I had to scramble with the help of the Day Surgery nurses to find another company that would take us back to The Grove. We were successful and returned at 7 pm.

I have decided to keep him in bed, just for comfort reasons, for the healing process. In bed, he is unencumbered with restrictive clothing, which is a good thing. Thankfully with the hospital bed one can adjust head and leg elevation so that, along with the PSW's repositioning him, we tried our best to keep him as comfortable as possible. Teresa, his companion, came in to visit mornings and I came and fed him lunch, spent the afternoon and after supper, with him settled for the night, returned home. Saturday morning, March 30, since there is a crackle in his chest, it was decided to get him up and into his wheelchair. That same day, at 6 pm it was recommended that he go to hospital for x-rays and intravenous antibiotics. We stayed in emergency Saturday until Monday morning. I returned home briefly during that time.

Dehydration, kidney failure, heart arrhythmia, sepsis infection throughout his body all indicated that his body was slowly shutting down. Amy and Rod visited and we continued contact with Jonathan.

April 2019 ♥

We returned to The Grove, for palliative care, Monday, April 1. They brought in a cot for me and provided meals and refreshments for us. They were very kind and thoughtful, checking on him and providing him with pain medications whenever he displayed signs of stress. He held our hands tightly and looked peaceful as we shared stories and music to comfort him. Jonathan arrived Wed. April 3 and the family was together until 10pm when they left, not wishing to see their father pass.

John passed peacefully in his sleep at 1:30am April 4, 2019.
He chose a long goodbye. Each day was a blessing.

After thought

I originally had two purposes for sharing this story… one to provide a therapeutic relief for myself, getting my thoughts and worries out of my head and onto paper. That was accomplished. Writing helped me look more objectively at each situation and step back emotionally, enabling me to rethink each day more rationally. The second purpose was, to give comfort to others starting this journey. I am not sure if I have helped or scared the dickens out of you. Either way this exposure to life is an enriching experience and when it is someone you love, there are no limits in responding to their needs. We can always see the precious soul in each one.

Advice

Take care of yourself and find the joy and humor experienced by your partner and the others walking the same path. Keep all your friends and when an invitation is extended to you, accept it, even if you would rather stay home and feel sorry for yourself, life goes on and that is what your partner would wish for you.

These words came to me in the middle of the night:

> He stood beside the door
> So quietly there,
> He looked at me
> I looked at him
> I didn't want to stare.
> There was a magic in it
> I felt I knew him from before.
> In that first glance
> I seemed drawn to him

Both hesitant
Not wanting to take a chance.

The moments became hours
The hours turned to days
The life we had together
Flew by, in such a haze.
If there is a "do over"
I'd love him once again.
Now the story's ending
Our lives, we chose to share,
I am so very thankful,
I saw him standing there.

As music comforted him, I selected special ones, for his memorial, with pictures, throughout the years.

Amazing Grace: Gary Downey
All Is Well With My Soul: Audrey Assad
Be still and Know I'm With You: The Fray
To Where You Are: Josh Groban
Angel: Sarah McLachlan
I Will Remember You: Sarah McLachlan
If We Ever Meet Again: Elvis Presley
Tears in Heaven: Eric Clapton
Hallelujah: Violin: Roy and Rosemary
It's A Wonderful World: Louis Armstrong
Angel Flying Too Close To the Ground: Willi Nelson
From A Distance: Bette Midler

A resident, Gerry: Observing the snow storm outside, I said," "just think I have to drive home in this"…His response. "And they tell me I'm crazy".

A resident, Linda: I said to her, "this is Father Michael, he is a priest, so you can confess to him anytime you like." Her response, "Don't do nothin' in here, nothin' to confess"

A couple, both residents: Paula turned to Tony, her husband and said, "You look very nice to-day" His response "Why thank you." she continued, "Yes, you could pass for 89".

I put on German music each night and when John could walk, we would dance across the room, maneuvering him toward the bed. I would sing off key to see if he would notice and one night he said as clear as could be, "You're crazy"…absolutely true wouldn't have it any other way….

The sweetness, innocence and unpredictability were so special, each day was an adventure. I called it dinner theater. When life hands you lemons, you really have to make lemonade. (Elbert Hubbard)

He chose a long goodbye. Each day was a blessing and I wouldn't have missed it for the world.